# From McComb
# to Jerusalem

## The Life Story of
## Irene (Shaloma) Levi

By Petra van der Zande

Unless otherwise stated, Scripture quotations are taken from THE
HOLY BIBLE, NEW INTERNATIONAL VERSION.

Cover picture: Petra van der Zande

ISBN  978 965 91615 4 6

Printed by LULU.com

*Summary:*
Authorized Biography of Irene Levi

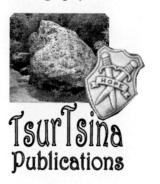

Tsur Tsina
Publications

website: http://christinaboerma.com/christinaboerma

Email: tsurtsinapublications@gmail.com

This book is dedicated to

the People of Israel

whom I have come to serve,

those mentioned in this book

and the ones that I forgot to mention!

# About the Cover

The Golden Gate, on the eastern side of the Temple Mount in Jerusalem, features prominently among Jews, Christians and Muslims as the place of the Last Judgment. In ancient times, judgments were rendered in the gates of the city (Gen. 19:1, 23:10). Since the Messiah was to come from the East (Matthew 24:27, Luke 19:35-38), it was concluded that his judgment would be at the eastern gate. In the assumption that the dead in the immediate vicinity will be the first to be raised, Muslims, Christians, and Jews want to be buried as close as possible to this gate.

According to Jewish tradition, the Shekhinah (שכינה) (Divine Presence) used to appear through this gate, and will appear again when the Messiah comes (Ezekiel 44:1–3). Then, a new gate will replace the present one now called *Sha'ar Harachamim* (שער הרחמים), the **Gate of Mercy.**

Christians believe that Jesus passed through this gate on Palm Sunday and upon His second coming, will enter the city through this gate. (Zechariah 14:4-5.)

Muslims call it the *Bab el-Dahariyeh* - **Gate of Eternity**, recalling the visions of Joel 4:2 and 12, or the **Twin Gate**, because of its shape.

In Biblical times, the gate was known as the **Beautiful Gate** (Acts 3:2,10.) It probably also existed during the period of Aelia Capitolina (Roman Period).

The cover picture shows the Kidron Valley and part of Jerusalem's Old City Wall with the Golden Gate. The writer took it from the direction of the Mount of Olives.

# Introduction

**Dear Reader,**

'Wheels Within Wheels and my Middle-East Whirl' had been an alternative title for this book. God's Living Spirit has led me in many down-to-earth ways, and like Ezekiel's wheels (read Ezekiel 1:1-21), I often felt as if He lifted me up, touching lives 'above the earth', to receive eternal blessings.

My personal 'whirl' through Middle-East countries was quite something. God led me to Lebanon, Turkey, Cyprus, Syria, Jordan, Iraq and mostly, Israel. He specifically called me to her capital, Jerusalem, the navel of the world, from where life comes forth. It was here that I have seen most of His faithfulness.

This book tells the story of my life. May the glory go to the 'Man upon the throne'.

I also like to express my thanks to Petra, for her amazing patience and ingenuity.

Irene (Shaloma) Levi

Jerusalem, February 2011

At the age of 19 and 91

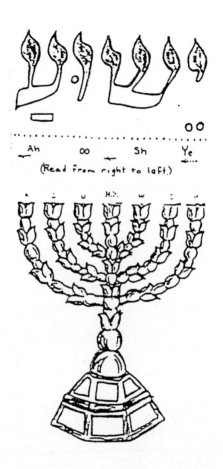

I always carry copies of this card in my purse, and whenever I can, tell people that **YESHUA** is the Light of Israel.

# CONTENTS

# CONTENTS

# CONTENTS

# PART 1

# 1919 - 1947

# 1

## 'The Place' Called Home

McComb, the town where I was born, sounds like the Hebrew *Makome*, meaning 'The Place'. In Biblical writings God is often called 'The Place'. I can testify that from this humble birthplace and every other place I lived, God has taken care of me.

My parents gave me two first names- Agnes (lamb) and Irene (peace). Later I learned that my family name "Poe" sounds like *Poh*, which is Hebrew for "here". Stringing all three together, the result was amazing ~ "By the Lamb, I have peace, here." It was like a prophecy of what my life in God was to be.

I was born in 1919 in McComb, Ohio, as the second child of John Stanley and Olive Poe. Together with my four sisters – Carol, Mary, Edna and Alice, we lived on a big 350 acre farm. Animals were raised for meat, chickens provided eggs and beehives gave us honey. We had to milk the cows, feed the pigs, watch sheep shearing and help lambs drink from bottles. Together with our faithful Collie dog, Laddie, we watched the cows graze by the sides of the road. During the harvest, we helped out by hoisting sheaves and watched the threshing of grain. We also tapped trees to collect sap for maple syrup.

My father, who was related to the famous poet Edgar Allan Poe, was also a writer. His exciting stories about my parents' trip out west, where he was born, were published in the town's newspapers. Dad loved his children and one day he gathered all five of his girls and held us up to be photographed. "I wouldn't take a million dollars for one of my girls," he said, "but wouldn't give five cents for another!"

In the evenings, after farm work and chores were done, as a family we sometimes sat in the kitchen, eating popcorn. Dad played the accordion and

Our farmhouse in McComb, Ohio.

Carol and me.

Playing in Mom and Dad's old car.

Before the last daughter was born.

hoped that one day his girls would play musical instruments in harmony. My sister Carol also played the accordion, I learned to play the violin and several of us took piano lessons as well.

Even though Dad paid for our hymn books, he didn't attend church, so Mum drove the big car to the nearest country church with us girls, usually traipsing in late. I loved to listen to the sermons and Sunday school stories and to participate in children's summer programs. Seeds of faith were sown during those years, but what touched me most was listening to the missionaries' stories of how "heathen" people became born again believers. When it became too intense, I had to go to the car and cry my heart out.

"Jerusalem! Jerusalem! Lift up your gates and sing!" No one in church could sing "The Holy City" as beautifully as Aunt Naomi. I never could have imagined that, one day, the Lord would call me to serve Him in Jerusalem.

Growing up in a rural area meant having to do without many luxuries. The kitchen sink had a pump but water for the rest of the house had to be drawn from the outside pump. There was no electricity either. Every day, lamps had to be trimmed and filled. Despite all the hard work, we had a lot of fun, and were blessed with good neighbors. I remember Faye Ewing singing "Whispering Hope" while we lay on our hillside. We were thrilled with all the songs we heard.

Until The Great Depression, which created havoc in the United States, life had been good to our family. But then, in 1930, when I was only ten, my father was killed in a tragic farm-related accident.

"God will take care of you!" the congregation sang while we sat in the city's Methodist church during the funeral service. My thirty-three-year-old father had been a loved and respected man, and from all over the countryside people came to pay their respects.

"Oh, girls!" my distraught mother wailed. "What will we do?"

After having cried nonstop for three days, determined to keep the family together, she composed herself. Mom dedicated her life to caring for her girls. An exceptional homemaker, she cooked noodles and bread, made jellies and butter, pickles and sauerkraut, and canned other foods galore. The garden provided vegetables and required disciplined labor. Mom knew how to make things from scratch. She also sewed clothes for the whole family, and that included our dolls.

Despite her extremely busy life, Mom found time to develop her cultural side as well. She played the piano, gave many readings by heart and was active in a book critique club.

For a time, the big farm was kept running with hired hands, but eventually it became too much for Mom. Our next home was in McComb, at the edge of town. I spent much of my time at the farm of my beloved Grandma and Grandpa Smith. They lived near our church and we drove there by horse and buggy. Grandma was a God-fearing woman. While she worked on her quilts, I read the large picture Bible. She created one quilt for each of us. Mine featured a Star of David. Often I played the piano and sang, "He Keeps Me Singing!"

As I was singing hymns, while out in the woods, I could feel God's presence. My dear grandparents also spoke German, which wasn't a popular language during Hitler's time. Later I wished I had learned to speak German.

In order to support the family, Mom had no choice but to find odd jobs outside the home. We girls used to see who could remember the greatest number of positions she had held. Finally she got steady work at the post office. Aunt Mae came to live with us, helping to care for the family. All of us girls went to school on foot, and we attended the Methodist church. Only after all her girls had left home did Mom remarry.

During one of my vacations, I had a summer job at the Collingwood farm, and was deeply moved by the godliness of the family who owned it.

"Would you like to join us, Irene?" Darius and Bernice asked. "We're going to Heers' Mission." I listened intently to Mr. Heers, and was moved to deep prayer as we sang, "Oh! I Want to See Him!"

It was here that I was introduced to a 'tabernacle chart'. Later in life, I created a copy of it on a large piece of cloth and often used it as a teaching tool.

Singing hymns increased my heavenward focus. One morning I was on my knees scrubbing the floor, and singing, "...almost persuaded, almost - but lost...." A shock went through me. "That's me!" I whispered. "How can I spend all the rest of my life knowing I'm lost and going to hell?"

I was even tempted to go to the farmer's barn and commit suicide. Thank God, I didn't have enough courage to do it!

One of Dad's handiworks - our merry-go-round.

Mom as a widow, taking care of her five daughters.

Last picture before the 'dispersion' of all five Poe-sisters.

# 2

## Hope and Salvation – Even for Me!

At school I was involved in religious exercises and delivered the valedictorian speech at graduation. Thanks to my excellent grades, in 1937 I was awarded a scholarship. I chose to study at Bluffton, the Mennonite College in Ohio, where one of my sisters had been. This college traditionally performed Handel's "Messiah" at Christmastime. My love affair with this beautiful Scriptural composition has lasted a lifetime.

Near the college was a missionary church, where I listened to young people giving their testimonies. I wanted to be saved too, but wondered if that was really possible. How much should I repent? And did I believe enough? Even though I didn't have the assurance that *my* sins were forgiven, I still longed to help people come to faith in Christ. Because of fear of man and the fact that I thought it would be impossible to stop fighting with my sisters, I had never responded to altar calls back in my home church.

That particular night, when the usual altar call came, I felt I had to go forward. I confessed to the preacher, "I don't think there's hope for me. I've tried before."

"Who do you think put that desire in your heart to be saved?" the preacher gently asked me.

It was then that I realized that God called *me* more than I wanted Him. *Is My Word not enough?* God spoke to my heart. *When Jesus said on the cross, 'It is finished!' that's when your salvation was accomplished.* There was no 'great vision of light', but God opened my eyes.

"I believe!" I simply confessed before a few believers. Now I knew for certain that my sins were forgiven, and that one day, I would go to Heaven. God had become real to me.

"My life is Yours, God!" I whispered as I walked home. The Holy

Spirit filled my heart to overflowing with a joy that lasted for days.

Even though Mom had us baptized by sprinkling after Dad had been killed, now that I truly believed, I wanted to obey the Bible. Immersion is an act by which the believer proclaims that his or her sins have been forgiven. It was in a stone quarry that I symbolically buried my old life in the watery grave. I was eighteen years old when, by God's grace, I was resurrected to a new life in Him.

"How can you know you're saved and going to Heaven when you die?" was one of the many questions the dormitory girls at college asked me. I radiated a joy that came from within and the Holy Spirit gave me the words to explain the way to salvation. While sharing what Jesus did for us on the cross and how we should repent and accept, I realized, "These students are now my mission field!"

"Wait till ten years from now," one of the students challenged me. "By then you will have forgotten all this!"

My life-long journey with the Lord has proven this girl's prediction wrong.

During another summer vacation I worked at the Fenbergs', a Jewish home in Findlay, where I learned of their customs. We kept in touch with each other, even after I moved to Israel.

My watery grave.

18

# 3

## The Importance of the Master's Decree

While war clouds gathered above Europe, I finished at Bluffton College. In September of 1939, the Second World War began with the invasion of Poland by Nazi Germany. America wanted to stay out of the conflict but nevertheless assisted Britain with arms.

I was blessed by directing a summer Bible camp for children in under-privileged surroundings in Frakes, Kentucky. About this time, a friend told me about Chicago Evangelistic Institute (CEI). For one year I had Bible training and precious fellowship there. I also helped out in the slum areas of Chicago.

Riding the El-trains (elevated trains, or overhead railroad) back and forth to my Oak Park residence, I was aware that many people were attacked while approaching the trains. So, each time I rode the train, I prayed, "Lord, let one start up with me and I'll see how Your Gospel will overcome!" I was protected by the most efficient security system– the power of God. Thugs never came near me.

Because of my desire to become a missionary/teacher, I thought it was important to get a teaching degree. I was able to board with my sister Carol who lived in Toledo, Ohio, and attend university there. During the two years I stayed in Toledo, I naturally helped out with my sister's household chores and taking care of their three children. She had given birth to twins – David and Donna, and was glad for the help. One day I decided to polish the wooden kitchen floor differently. I put one of the children on a large cloth, and pulled him around. A photo of a parade we organized for the neighborhood's many children was once published in a Toledo newspaper.

While continuing my university studies toward my Bachelor of Science in Education, I worked night shifts at a factory making shells for the war effort.

Everyone had to pitch in, as an increasing volume of weapons was needed. The Japanese attack on Pearl Harbor had forced America to join the steadily spreading conflict.

Reinhard Heydrich's 'Final Solution' had been set in motion. News of Jewish mass murders was strongly denounced in London, Washington and Moscow. But the Allied Forces were too busy fighting a war to do anything about it. "Accelerate the 'Final Solution'!" Hitler ordered his willing helpers.

Despite the war, civilians tried to go about their daily business. I finished my Bachelor Studies in 1943 and began teaching in a suburb of Detroit, Michigan. The majority of pupils were African-Americans, which I felt was good preparation for future missionary teaching. I volunteered with the National Association for the Advancement of Colored People (NAACP), and felt inclined to visit their churches and to befriend the colored teachers in our school. During that time, there was still segregation of blacks and whites.

In 1945, my days were filled to the brim! During the day I taught first and second grades, and volunteered at a Baptist church, where I played my violin and helped with youth fellowships and home visitations. The evenings were filled working for my Master's degree in Educational Administration at Wayne University in Detroit. At every meeting of professors, advisors or fellow graduate students, I always found opportunities to speak about the Lord. Although I received my Master's Degree, I felt that the *Decree* of the Master was far more important!

Finally, the long awaited VE Day (Victory Europe) arrived on May 8, 1945. Ecstatic people took to the streets, laughing, shouting and hugging each other. Thousands also had to face their personal losses - sons, husbands and fathers. World War II had ended, but the survivors were to carry physical and mental scars for the rest of their lives.

Because I now had Bible College and teaching degrees, I was able to teach Bible in Virginia's public schools through a national program. I felt that God wanted me to take this step in faith since there was no salary, only what local churches provided.

In post-war America, it was difficult to receive permission to buy a car, so I had to use public transportation. One morning I rushed to catch the bus when I realized my purse was still at home. "Well," I reasoned, "I always tell the children that His Word has an answer for *everything*." I opened my Bible and, lo and behold, there were some dollars inside - enough to pay my bus fare! During an evening service someone had given me the money and I'd forgotten I put it there.

Despite being a qualified teacher holding a Master's degree, I lived on the little support I received. I taught Bible in eight schools. Fifth graders learned from the Old Testament, while the sixth graders studied the New Testament. All of the children chose to attend, and classes were coordinated with subjects their regular teachers taught.

"Here comes Miss Poe, the Bible teacher," the children sing-songed. Years later, I was to learn that *Mispo* in Hebrew was food given to camels. Of course I hoped that my 'camels' had been well fed from His Word.

But not only children needed to hear about the Lord. Through special programs and plays, and through the students' personal notebooks, we also reached the parents by showing them what we had taught their children. At one place we had a play about Elijah. Red paper resembled the fire, which then 'fell' on the altar we built on stage.

During summer vacation, Lenora Christy and I started many Daily Vacation Bible School (D.V.B.S.) groups in many places in Virginia. My contacts with the Christy family continued, even to this day.

Even after VJ (Victory Japan) Day on August 14, 1945, American soldiers continued to be sent to the Far East. The army base in Alexandria, Virginia, where I lived, provided quite a lot of excitement to the area. During my stay there I became attracted to wonderful, believing men. In Fort Belvoir, one of my teaching locations, I worked with a Wednesday night church meeting. I corresponded for months with a soldier who was sent to the Far East. He was a true man of God who did missionary work in his spare time.

Then one night, I had a dream: I saw Jesus, dressed in everyday clothes, sitting amidst a circle of friends. When I woke up the next morning, I came to a startling realization – "It is Jesus I love in these servants of God!" I knew it was Jesus because of His eyes.

During the summer, I worked at an all-night coffee shop, which was often crowded with soldiers who frequently flirted with me. While witnessing to them, I remembered Jesus' eyes from my dream, and in faith, 'saw' God's Word coming alive in their lives.

I felt happy in Virginia, and even in the nearby Washington, D.C. Bible study groups which I attended. However, it wasn't exactly a foreign mission field. I knew it was time to move on!

# 4

## A Growing Love for the Jewish People

New York City was the place for me to look into foreign missions. Substitute teaching was providing me with an income. The year was now 1946 and more and more, I began to hear of the needs in India. However, I kept meeting Jewish people everywhere. Figuring it would always come in handy, I took a few lessons in Hebrew and Yiddish at the Cohen Mission. At the central church I attended, I led children's "Our J.O.Y. Hour" (Jesus first, Others next, Yourself last). I also helped Mr. Birnbaum there in his strategic outreach to his people by printing large-print verses of scriptures and notices in Hebrew, which I couldn't yet read.

God used evolving world events to open my eyes to the fact that Old Testament prophecies were being fulfilled, as were those in the New Testament! And I had been teaching them both in the Virginia schools!

"That's not for us Jews!" was often the Jewish reaction when I shared my insights. Not wanting to give them the impression I was introducing them to some foreign religion, I responded, "But don't you see? You're the ones who should be speaking to me! It was you, the Jews, who gave me the Scriptures!" I felt the same sorrow God and Paul must have felt. These were the ones He had chosen to be His witnesses. (Through them Messiah came.) But instead of being givers, they were the unwilling recipients.

In New York I met several Jewish women who were to have a great impact on my life. Through them, a deep love for the Jewish people began to grow. Olive Lucas was a street preacher. I was amazed at the way this brave woman handled verbal 'stonings' from the gathering crowd, and at her ever-so-tender responses. Spending time with this godly woman strengthened my yearning for Jews to know their loving Messiah.

A Jewish believer, Carmen Lyons, gave Bible studies on the book of Ruth. I strongly identified with the way Ruth, the Moabitess, clung to her mother-in-law, Naomi, the Jew. I also loved the book of Romans, which I began to study and memorize.

A lady speaker invited me to attend a talk at a Christian college and gave me a front row seat. She had prepared a certain subject, but changed it at the last moment. Instead, she felt led to speak on Romans 11. "Through your mercy, they may obtain mercy," she quoted and expounded from Romans 11.

*Where are You leading me, eventually, Lord?* I wondered.

In New York I helped Ruth and Esther Angel, Hilda Kozier and others in their outreach to Jewesses. But there were also Charles Cline, Solomon Birnbaum and other men who were boldly sharing the Truth on the streets. I joined them by praying for them and distributing leaflets.

During a conference organized by Charles Feinberg on Jewish evangelism, a Canadian believer with whom I fellowshipped said to me, "God is calling you among the Jews." She donated her typewriter, which I would use extensively for years.

Then, at a Youth for Christ meeting, a lady sitting next to me said, "God has given you a love for the Jews."

*How does she know?* I thought. *Shouldn't every believer love the Jewish people?*

Samuel Needleman had a mission in New York's Lower East Side. Due to the fact that he was getting older and weaker, the place had become rundown.

"If you let me stay there," I suggested, "I will straighten it up for you." I liked the fact that it even had a storefront window.

The first morning there, I woke up with the following titles, 'Rahab's Grace'; 'Rebecca's Gems'; 'Rachel's Glory' and 'Ruth's Gleanings'. These words inspired me to write four poems. Each poem was part of my calling. Written out on small, decorated posters, the poems were displayed, in turn, in the mission's front window. Inside the mission building I arranged chairs in a circle and conducted Bible studies, which Jewish immigrants, who happened to come by, began to attend. Some were Holocaust survivors who had chosen to build new lives in America.

In those days, India and Mahatma Gandhi, and their struggle for independence were much in the news. After meeting and helping a missionary couple from India, I was convinced that those millions of Indian people needed to know Jesus' love.

## RAHAB'S GRACE
Joshua ~ type of Jesus as Deliverer ~
Joshua 2:6

They were considered spies,
though the land belonged to them.
Then Joshua came to Canaan
to bring Israel in again.

Rahab showed them mercy
Harlot though she be
She sheltered them within her house
Lest Satan's hosts should see.

She recognized the Jews' One God,
The Lord of all creation,
Was still the Mighty One to save
Her with the Jewish nation.

By a cord they made escape
Through this Gentile's window
"Wilt **thou** be hid for three sad days
To the Mountain thou shalt then go."

"This scarlet cord which saved us Jews
From the pursuer's face,
When thou shalt in thy window bind
'Twill save **you** by **our** grace."
So Joshua saved this Rahab
And Joshua saved the Jews
Whenever God saves anyone
The scarlet line He'll use.

Jesus is "Joshua" – Savior
Leads out of sin to His Land
The scarlet line, His precious Blood.
Written with God's own Hand….

Hang it in your life's window.
To save God's "spies" and you
When the Trumpet sounds
and this world falls Christ takes
His saved ones through.

## REBEKAH'S GEMS
Isaac ~ type of Christ the Sons, seeking a
Bride ~ believers ~ through the Holy
Spirit. Genesis 24.

I am the Father's servant,
You are kind to give me to eat,
But first I must tell you my errand
To make this journey complete.

My Master is wondrously wealthy,
And he has an only Son.
To Him He has given all things
And unto His chosen one.

You are the one He has chosen
To become his bride today.
Are you willing to leave all and follow,
To meet him at the end of the way?

My Master said, "Go to My kindred;
The angel shall prosper thee there.
If the called one be not willing to follow,
Thou art free; but this time my Son spare."

Behold these gems and this raiment,
The Son has riches untold!
There is nothing His bride shall be wanting,
And His love is a jewel of gold.

Oh, Rebekah, don't keep Him waiting;
He longs to own you right now
Thy family will give you their blessing
As they see how blessed **art** thou.

And oh, the journey's not tiresome,
You'll soon see the One you adore.
You'll light off your camel to meet Him
While He greets you as His
evermore!

### EVEN SO, COME QUICKLY,
### LORD JESUS!

## RACHEL'S GLORY

Joseph ~ type of Christ as Beloved Son and forgiving Brother; rejected, then exalted. Genesis 37-50.

Rachel's one main glory
Was hidden in her son
Of all of Israel's children,
He was the chosen one.

The other sons of Jacob
Were jealous of Joseph's state
They sold him into Egypt
Thus to vent their hate.

Later Joseph fed them
When they came down for corn.
How he longed to enlighten, forgive them
And again with his family be one.

In fullness of time, in his glory
Yet his heart running over with tears,
He revealed himself to his brethren
And his life and love through those long years.

So Rachel had one chief glory,
Like Mary, the Lord Jesus' mother.
My one main glory ~ to show Israel's seed
Their Savior, Christ Jesus ~
**their Brother!**

**GOD**

**MAN**

**the GOD~MAN
Messiah ~ Christ**

*Coming soon to reign!*

## RUTH'S GLEANINGS

Boaz ~ type of Christ as Kinsman Redeemer. Book of Ruth, esp. Chapter 2

I'm just a Gentile believer,
I've come to the God of the Jews,
Forsaken my old life in "exile"
To live where my God shall choose.

I hear that you Jews love strangers,
That you let them glean in your fields;
Already you're dropped
handfuls on purpose
And I've had such bounteous yields.

Such gleanings from sacred pages
The Jews have let fall for me:
These sheaves from which
I'm now gleaning
Are all so fruitful and free!

Why, O Naomi's Kinsman,
Shouldst thou take knowledge of me
Seeing I am a stranger
And not of Israel like thee?

A full reward Thou hast given,
O Lord God of Israel!
As under Thy wings I'm now trusting,
Here all's so abundantly well.

At last I am one with Thy people
Through Thee
Who alone couldst redeem,
O Israel's great Kinsman,
my Bridegroom,
Forever together we'll glean!

# 5

## A 'Damascus Road Experience' in Oklahoma

Since the foundation of Wycliffe Bible Translators in 1942, hundreds of teams now worked to translate the Bible, or parts of it, into every living language. Their Summer Institute of Linguistics (S.I.L) was based in Oklahoma. Because of my perceived calling to India, I felt I might need their summer course, which I attended in 1947. I was able to earn my keep by performing household duties for couples.

Even though there were special prayer times for many countries, none was set aside to pray for the Jewish people. It troubled my friend and me. "Does no one care?" we wondered.

It was in Oklahoma that I had a completely new experience ~ a heavy burden of prayer for Jerusalem fell upon me. Night after night, leaving my friends, I was overcome with a burden similar to what Paul must have felt. While I interceded for the city of God, it felt as if I were torn in two. "What are You trying to tell me, LORD?" I cried.

Ironing was one of my household duties, and I often worked with an open Bible on the ironing board. I loved the book of Romans so much that I continued to commit it to memory. When I reached chapter 11, I was deeply touched when I grasped the truth - God had not rejected His People. They didn't stumble so far as to fall beyond recovery. Because of their transgression – rejecting Messiah - salvation had come to the Gentiles to make Israel jealous. And if their loss meant riches for the Gentiles, how much greater riches would be their fullness! Their acceptance would be life from the dead.

As a Gentile believer, I had been grafted in as a wild olive shoot, and was now nourished and supported by the sap of the root, the Truth of God, begun in the Old Testament!

"Oh the depth of the riches of the wisdom and knowledge of God!

How unsearchable His judgments…!" I began to weep and fell on my knees next to the ironing board. I literally felt God's hand on my head.

The end of the Wycliffe summer course was in sight and I waited for God to tell me where to go next. "Do you want me to return to New York City?" I prayed. "Lord, please let the speaker have a word for me. I need a confirmation of my calling. What specific thing do I need to do when I leave here?"

That particular day, at the closure of the course, I had been memorizing Romans 15 and to my surprise, the speaker read that same chapter. Then came verse 25, "**Now, I go to Jerusalem in the service of the saints there…**"

Exactly at that moment, across the hall someone raised a window shade, flooding the place where I sat with a glaring light. To me, it was a 'Damascus Road experience' as powerful as the one experienced by the apostle Paul.

God answered my prayers – I knew that He was calling me to Jerusalem!

# PART 2

# 1947 - 1948

# 6

## Can a Nation be Born in a Day?

On November 29, 1947, in New York the UN General Assembly voted to divide Palestine into Jewish and Arab States, with Jerusalem as an international zone. The British Mandate would officially end on May 15, 1948. Around the world, the Jews rejoiced in their future statehood but the Arab countries and the Arab League refused to recognize the resolution.

After the Wycliffe course, I had returned to New York City and told my friends not only about my calling to Jerusalem but also to the Jewish people, who were longing for a homeland. (See Appendix for Israel's history.)
The year 1948 turned out to be a very important year for Israel as well as for me. January first, I received my brand new American passport. "T h a n k You, Lord!" I leafed through the empty pages. "You are leading me one step at a time. Now I need a visa to Palestine." Eventually, I would get there, but via a God-ordained detour.

A friend in Washington, D.C. did her best to get me a visa for Jerusalem. When she didn't succeed, she suggested, "You'd better apply for a visa to Lebanon, and from there travel overland to Jerusalem."
"We'd like to support you with $200 a month," offered the River Rouge congregation where I fellowshipped in the Detroit area, when they heard about my calling to the Middle East.
"If you need a mission board, we'd be honored to become your Board of Directors," two well-known New York gentlemen offered.
"Hm." I thought about it for a moment. "You think I need one? For now, I don't think so." I smiled at my friends. "Thanks anyhow!"
The day of departure was rapidly approaching.
"There's a gentleman here who'd like to speak with you, Irene," some-

one told me.

"How do you do?" The tall, quiet gentleman had an obvious British accent. "It's my first time in the States, and I just heard that you are planning to leave for the Middle East." He smiled at me. "I've been working there for over ten years now, and thought you might like to have some addresses."

"That's nice of you," I responded. "Thank you, Mr. Duce."

The same day that British High Commissioner Cunningham left Palestine, May 15, 1948, David Ben Gurion declared the statehood of Israel. The miracle was already foretold in Isaiah 66: 8. "Who has ever heard of such a thing? Who has ever seen such thing? Can a **country be born in a day**, or can a nation be brought forth in a moment?" May 15, the newborn state was attacked by six Arab armies – Egypt, Syria, Transjordan, Lebanon, Saudi Arabia and Iraq.

"The value of Jerusalem cannot be measured, weighed or counted," Prime Minister Ben-Gurion said. "If a country has a soul, then Jerusalem is the soul of the land of Israel… Our enemies know that the fall of Jerusalem would be a mortal blow for all the Jewish people."

It was a terrible blow when on May 28, 1948, the Jewish Quarter of Jerusalem's Old City fell to the Jordanian Legion. At first, it seemed the Arabs were going to drive the Palestinian Jews into the sea, as they had threatened. However, much to their surprise, the Jews began to counter attack and even gain victories over their multiple enemies.

*Ein brerah* – no choice, was what spurred the Israelis on.

# 7

## Toward the Promised Land

**June 11, 1948.**

I stood among the crowd on the quay of New York's Harbor, anxious to board the S.S. *Marine Carp*. I envied the Jews who held Israeli entry visas and were to disembark at Haifa. On this voyage there were also many American Jews going to help Israel fight their War of Independence. "Machalniks" they were called. (*Midnadvay Chutz La'aretz* - Volunteers from Abroad.)

Believing it was the safest way to travel, my friends had bought me a first class ticket. My luggage consisted of teaching materials, a portable phonograph, a mess kit, supplies and clothes.

From the first class deck, I waved good-bye to my friends standing on the quay. One of them was Bill Krill, who had been a close friend. While traveling together on the New York subways, we often sang and purposely talked about the Gospel, hoping people would listen in on our conversation. One day, Bill had even asked me to marry him. "Bet you're going to marry someone British over there," Bill had offered. But I was too busy serving the Lord to even think about getting married.

After waving one last time, I went to the cabin I shared with a Jewish lady.

"*Leila tov* – good night," Miss Gottlieb said before turning off the light.

Not knowing anyone on board, I felt odd among the first class passengers. *I don't belong here,* I thought and began to mingle with the Jews occupying the lower decks. Soon, I was able to sing along with their many Hebrew songs.

I finally met a fellow believer, and together we prayed for the people on board. Moshe was a young man, one of a pair of twins, who allowed us to pray for him. I believe he ultimately came to faith in Yeshua. Later I heard that Moshe was killed in battle shortly after landing.

New York -
Friends seeing me off.

Moshe, who was later killed.

En route to Lebanon
and proudly holding
my Bible with the Star
of David!

*S.S. Marine Carp.*

While the *Marine Carp* sailed along, I enraptured the passengers of the lower decks with the music of Händel's *Messiah*. The powerful *Hallelujah Chorus* touched many hearts and I had to play the music over and over again on the portable phonograph.

When the ship approached the harbor near Athens, Greece, Jewish passengers were waiting en masse to do some sightseeing. Much to their chagrin, they were told to stay on board.

"Why aren't we allowed off the ship?" the disgruntled Jewish passengers demanded to know. "Why can't we visit Piraeus?"

"Because you're at war!" the Greek authorities told them.

I felt someone should break the disappointment and grabbed my chance. "I'll tell you about something that happened in Athens! Ever hear about a Jew named Paul? He spoke to the people of Athens about their statue of an 'unknown' God." Nobody seemed to object to me telling a New Testament story ending with the true God.

As the ship continued its journey, I noticed that the non-Jews on board kept mostly to the upper decks. Among them I found a believer from Syria who shared my vision to try to reach the many children on board. We agreed that I would use my flannelgraph material to teach them from the Bible. After a few days I had another suggestion, "Why don't we act out the book of Esther?"

Placards were made, inviting all the passengers on board to attend the play. The Jewish passengers were amazed at the fact that Gentile children were dramatizing the Jewish story of Esther. It was a great success.

I shared my poem "Ruth's Gleanings" with the Jewish passengers when they gathered around and asked me all kinds of questions. Of course I was more than happy to answer them.

The two-week sea journey was coming to an end. Later, someone remarked that I had managed to pack more into the trip than many people would have done in a whole year. Before their disembarking in Haifa, I presented each of my new friends with a four-line poem relating to their Biblical names. In later years, I would meet several of these people in Jerusalem.

Longingly, I looked at the city of Haifa that seemed like a three-layered cake. In times long gone, at Mount Carmel Elijah's God had answered with fire. *Wish I could disembark here, instead of Beirut.* I sighed. My head snapped up when I heard a voice call, "Can someone help me get him down into the little boat?" A British officer stood next to a man on a stretcher.

"Here, let me help you!" I rushed to him. *This is my chance to get ashore!* flashed through my mind.

"No, you can't help me!" the officer brushed me off.

34

Suddenly afraid of the authoritative British officer, I kept quiet. I began to realize I couldn't leave the ship – my belongings were still in our cabin, including my Lebanese visa. Later, this experience helped me to feel sympathy for those Jews who had been prevented by the British officers from entering Mandate Palestine. Many had been turned away and sent to Cyprus' detention camps. Until the State of Israel was declared, many had languished there. Little did I know then that one day, I would live in Haifa, directing the Mount Carmel School nor that years later, I would be able to visit Cyprus and see those wretched camps.

As the ship continued its northern course toward Lebanon, I stood on deck. Struggling with a feeling of loss, I followed Israel's coastline. *Did I miss a God-given chance?* I wondered. *Lord, is Lebanon indeed part of Your plan for my life?*

# 8

## The Lord Is For Me, I Will Not Fear

Natalie Stevenson, whom I had met in New York, was on her way back to Baghdad, where she and her husband had a Christian ministry. She met me when I arrived in Beirut, and took me to Bhamdoun, north of Beirut.

I shared a room with Sumaya, the daughter of Shukrallah Naseef. The Arab barber was a believer, whose house was a 'home away from home'. With oriental hospitality, he also opened his home to Ibrahim, a former Muslim. Prayer and singing were always present in his home. While he shaved their beards or cut his clients' hair, Shukrallah shared the Gospel. "I always have a 'captive' audience!" he used to joke.

> In Biblical times, Lebanon played an important role as the provider of cedar wood for Solomon's Temple in Jerusalem. After the defeat of the Ottomans, Lebanon and Syria became a French Mandate. Most of the Lebanese Jews lived in Beirut and were free to practice their religion as they wished.

One of their neighbors was a refugee from Jaffa, Israel. During the War of Independence Naomi Kassis, her family and thousands of others had listened to the Arab leaders who urged them to flee. "You can return after we've driven the Jews into the sea," they were promised.

I befriended the humble believer, who was willing to translate and give me Arabic lessons. We began to have children's meetings, for which I used my flannelgraph to tell them Bible stories.

When I realized that Bhamdoun had a small Jewish community, one day I suggested to Naomi, "Let's go visit the rabbi's wife."

36

We were welcomed in with typical Middle Eastern hospitality. "So how did you end up here?" the rabbi's wife asked Naomi and listened with growing interest to her story. "I'm so sorry that you had to leave everything behind!" The Jewish woman was genuinely shocked when she heard about Naomi's plight.

"Oh, that's all right." Naomi smiled. "The Bible tells us that the Jews would come back to the Land."

"But how do you manage to live?"

"The Lord takes care of me wherever I am," Naomi said. "I'm also a nurse, so I can help others." Her eyes shone when she added, "And you know, the Bible says we can have a home in Heaven!"

During that visit, Yeshua was magnified, and it inspired me to write a midrash about it.

A *midrash* is a teaching derived through wordplay between the teacher's words and usually several biblical texts.

*"Most of the Arab refugees lost everything during the War of Independence. Because of their hardship, they could relate to Holocaust survivors, who had lost everything during WWII. Also, Ruth, the Moabitess, was doubly blessed because she clung to Naomi, returning to her land, and helping her. Like Ruth and Naomi, Jew and Arab could likewise fulfill their destinies."*

One day I came home to find Stanley sitting in Shukrallah's home. "Mr. Duce! I didn't expect to see you here!" I was genuinely surprised.

His full name was Stanley Joseph Duce. I learned that the Arabs didn't know the name "Stanley", so they called him "Yusif".

Because nobody except us spoke much English, Stanley and I began to intercede for the people among whom we were living and working. Usually, praying together brings people closer to each other. Gradually, a special bond began to grow between the two of us.

"I'd like to take you to Cedars of Lebanon in Ain Zhalta," Stanley invited me one day. The beautiful area, one of the largest cedar groves in Lebanon, was a perfect setting for Stanley. He asked me to marry him. I didn't accept. Hurt by my rejection, Stanley walked back down the trail alone, and left the area soon after this incident.

With Lebanon's independence, the Jewish community had expanded. Within Lebanon and Syria they were regarded as the most highly organized society. For decades, the Jews of Beirut had lived prosperous lives. When the birth of Israel infuriated Arab mobs, the Lebanese Christians protected their Jewish neighbors. In those times, Lebanon was a Christian 'lighthouse' in Scripture distribution.

I felt it was time to move on and rented a room in Beirut's Jewish quarter. Here, I began to visit their synagogues and homes, and befriended many. The Jews resembled the Lebanese people – warm, considerate, open to new ideas, intelligent and generous. Wherever I went, I shared about the "Greatest Jew Who let me in on the Treasure given first to the Jews".

I also had contact with the Christians in Beirut. While attending a church near the American University, I met Carrie Graves, a child evangelist. Because Carrie spoke fluent Arabic, the two of us decided to travel to Sidon and see if we could help the Palestinian Arabs living in a refugee camp.

With the arrival of a considerable number of Palestinian refugees during the Arab Exodus of 1948, most of the Sidonian Jews fled. The Palestinian Arabs were settled in large refugee camps – Ein El-Hilweh and Mia Mia. At first, the camps consisted of enormous rows of tents, but later, houses were constructed.

Near Sidon, we rented a room with a table. Our beds were two air mattresses. We set to work immediately. From the cloth we bought, we cut out shirts, shorts and whatever came to our minds. Mom had mailed instant soup, from which we cooked a kettle full. Soon, a long line of refugees formed, each holding cups, cans or whatever could hold a portion.

"You are invited to come and listen to a story," Carrie announced in Arabic.

Most of them were women, who sat on the floor in an adjacent building and listened to Carrie's message of God's love and hope for them. Expecting a stampede when the ready-to-sew clothes and yarn were to be handed out, Carrie and I decided to stand outside on the porch and give the items through an open window. As we had feared, because they had so little, most of the women tried to grab whatever they could. The 'hand out' experience was a strong contrast to the message that they had been quietly listening to just minutes before.

Carrie felt it was time for her to leave Beirut, but I knew I had to stay on in Sidon and wanted to find out if there were any Jews left in the city. One day I walked downhill, and stopped at the first kiosk.

"Can you tell me where the Jewish quarter is?" I inquired.

A Jewish family warmly welcomed me into their home and I wasn't there long, when a keffiyah-wearing Arab officer stormed into the house.

"Are you a Jew?" he yelled at me.

"No. But my Savior is a Jew!" I responded with my usual forthrightness.

"You come with me!" the officer commanded.

My answer somehow touched the heart of my newfound Jewish friend. "I'll go with you!" He accompanied me toward the police station.

"You go home now!" the officer told the Jewish man.

My heart sank. *What's going to happen, Lord?* I wondered.

The policeman guided me up some stairs to a room full of officers. They began to shout and debate in Arabic. I didn't understand a word of what they were saying and fear grabbed my heart.

"Do you mind if I pray over here?" I pointed to a quiet corner. I didn't know what else to do or say, or what to pray, but God knew my heart.

"Are you American? Where's your passport?" an officer demanded.

"In Mia Mia," I told him. I had not taken my purse along, and didn't have money for a return ride to the camp.

"Well, then we have to take you there to see it," one of the officers suggested.

*This is your way back to the camp!* the Lord spoke to my heart. He answered my prayer in a most unconventional way. My fear of these men was gone! I knew that my life was in His hands. Hemmed in by officers, and trying hard not to show my glee, I was driven back to Mia Mia Camp. *What will those refugees think when they see me enter with all those police officers?* I thought. *Perhaps they think I'm an important person? Or that I did something wrong!*

"What are you doing here?" one of the officers asked as the car entered the camp's narrow alleys.

"We're helping the refugees." I told them what we had been doing so far.

It seemed the officer began to look at me differently. The men followed me to our room.

An officer looked around the bare place. "You say that you are American?"

"Yes, I am. Here's my passport."

"Can't an American afford better than **this**?" He pointed to the only thing left in the room – one air mattress.

"To be rich in God is better than to be rich in goods," I responded and told him about the joy of life that comes from following the Savior, the Shepherd, and that serving others is part of that walk. Before they left, I handed each of the police officers a tract in Arabic.

I wasn't really in love with Stanley, but appreciated him for who he was. Not having a choice, Stanley learned to accept my feelings, and value my friendship.

Together, we went to visit several Jewish leaders in Beirut. Since the establishment of the Jewish state, Arab opposition and a strong anti-Israel sentiment had increased. Life wasn't easy for the Lebanese Jewish community.

Stanley was fluent in Arabic, and until then had mostly ministered to the Arab people. However, God had begun to show him His plan for the Jews and their return to Israel. I was pleased when he told me, "I think I should learn Hebrew as well."

Joseph Lichtman, son of a Lebanese Jewish rabbi, lived in Bhamdoun. Later he moved to Jerusalem where we met often. Joseph began to teach Stanley and me the Hebrew language. Studying the biblical language together bonded us even more.

Shukrallah's Barber shop and Ibrahim.

Bhamdoun - Naomi, me and Martha.

40

# 9

## Damascus, the City of Jasmine

Damascus, Syria, was only eighty kilometers away - a bus ride from Beirut. So one day I packed my bag, grabbed a handful of tracts someone had given me, and boarded the bus to Ash-Sham, the 'City of Jasmine'.

I peered through the dusty window of the bus at the scenery around me. There it was, Damascus. Like Jerusalem, the old city of Damascus was enclosed by thick walls, as the important city had been at a crossroads of major trade routes.

> Many Jews had been wealthy merchants and money-lenders, the bankers of the city. With the outbreak of the War of Independence, an intensified persecution of the Jewish population followed. Jewish property was confiscated and attempts to flee were harshly punished.

Upon arrival, I immediately went looking for a church someone had told me about. Here, I met an elderly Jewish believer who led me to the Jewish Quarter. We'd only spoken to a few shop owners and handed out some tracts, when a jeep screeched to a halt. It was the police.

"Get in!" the officer barked.

I didn't understand a word of what the two men were discussing. Neither did I grasp what was said in the many different offices we were taken to next. I had to wait outside while my Jewish friend was interrogated. I fervently prayed for him, and wondered what would happen.

"Come with us!"

I was taken to a big room with half a dozen officers. Sitting behind a big table was a stern looking man. "Now what is this paper that you were giving to the Jews?" The man held up a tract. "A Hebrew Search for the Blood of Atonement?"

"This explains the way of salvation through atonement by the blood of Jesus, His having died for our sins." I spoke with God-given courage. "Atonement and forgiveness came to all of us, by way of the Jews. This leaflet is to help them understand it."

"Oh well!" The officer leaned back in his chair. "If this is directed to them and their religion, never mind." He made a dismissive motion with his hand. "You can go."

For me, Lebanon had only been meant as a way station to Jerusalem. Shortly after the Damascus adventure, I felt it was time to get moving toward Jerusalem. Stanley had given me an address of a couple who were very much loved in the Middle East – Roy and Dora Whitman. They lived in Amman, Jordan. It wasn't Jerusalem, but I was getting closer.

More than 70% of the British Mandate of Palestine had been east of the Jordan River. The sparsely populated 'Transjordan' received independence in March of 1946. Abdullah became King of The Hashemite Kingdom of Jordan, with Amman as its capital.

# 10

## A Second Chance

It wasn't difficult to find the Amman address Stanley had given me. I rang the doorbell.

"Hello, I'm Irene Poe," I introduced myself and then blurted out in my mid-American enthusiasm, "Oh Dora! I'm so glad to meet you!"

"How do you do?" British Dora held out her hand.

The Whitmans helped me find a couple who lived in Zarqa, a village not far from Amman. Meggid and Selma Kawar belonged to a local assembly of believers. I shared a room with Mrs. Bashara Kawar. This lady was widely known for her heavenly revelations that were accompanied by a dove-shaped appearance in blood on her forehead. Mrs. Kawar spoke Arabic, and could be heard 'praying in tongues' - in many languages. Some of her recorded words had to do with the return of the Jews to their inheritance in the Land as well as to holy living.

I stared at the telegram that just had arrived from Beirut. "Shall I come?" Stanley asked.

Mrs. Kawar, spoke a little English. "This seems more than just a visit," she sweetly hinted. "It sounds more like a proposition."

*Whatever!* I thought. "Come!" I wired back.

Before Stanley's arrival, I participated in Dora's women's meeting where I explained my tabernacle chart with Arabic labels, and she translated. All of it was God's object lessons about the Savior Who was to come.

That autumn of 1948, I waited at the Whitmans' house in Amman for Stanley to arrive. Like Mrs. Kawar had predicted, Stanley again asked me to marry him. Between the first and second proposals, I had begun to notice Stanley's graciousness. I admired his experience and vast knowledge of the Middle East. The fact that he was accepted by earnest believers was also an important factor for me. God always gave His best to those who left the choice with Him. I knew God was giving me a treasure. This time, I agreed wholeheartedly.

Our engagement was celebrated with great joy in the Whitmans' home. Because of our desire to get married in Jerusalem, Stanley and I began making preparations to leave. I laughed when it dawned on me that my friend Bill had been right after all – I was going to marry an Englishman.

Our engagement in Amman.

# PART 3

# 1948 - 1950

# 11

## Jerusalem: The Navel of the World

A rented car was packed for the journey. Stanley and I said good-bye to our friends in Amman. We traveled an ancient route toward the Jordan River.

"This was the place where the Israelites crossed over into the Promised Land," Stanley told me.

Modern day travelers didn't have to wait for the waters to split, but could use a bridge that was named in honor of the commander-in-chief of the British forces – Lord Allenby.

The West Bank was now under control of The Hashemite Kingdom of Jordan. We traversed the broad, spacious valley in which Jericho, The City of Palms, lay and began the winding ascent into the Judean Wilderness. Not far from the biblical site of Ma'ale Adumim, I spotted a road sign, "The Inn of the Good Samaritan". For decades, the fortress-like building had been protecting travelers against robbers. Jesus' parable came alive before my eyes.

"There it is." Stanley pointed toward a distant mountain ridge. "Jerusalem!"

I looked at the landmarks of the Mount of Olives – the tower of the Church of the Ascension, the Augusta Victoria Hospital, and Mount Scopus University. It was my first of hundreds of trips UP to Jerusalem, the place to which God had called me.

The car slowed down when we reached the Mandelbaum Gate. The border post between Jordan and Israel was situated just north of the western edge of Jerusalem's Old City. Passing through the concrete and barbed wire barrier between the Israeli and Jordanian sectors, we stopped for passport inspection. Stanley had been in Jerusalem many times and knew his way around. He drove straight to Nablus Street – *Rehov Shechem* in Hebrew, and to St. George's Cathedral, where Bishop and Mrs. Stewart were then in charge.

After someone showed us to our rooms, we went down to meet the other guests. Several of them worked among Jews, but because of the fighting, had sought shelter at St. George's. Due to the Cathedral's position, it had sustained considerable damage. The roof and interior had suffered from constant shelling, and many of the stained glass windows were broken. We also saw that many buildings in the nearby American Colony were damaged as well.

In the evenings we joined the other guests who gathered around a kerosene heater to pray for the peace of Jerusalem. Everything was scarce in Jerusalem – water, food, heat, and electricity, but we learned to make do. Water used for washing was kept to flush the toilet.

"Any news yet?" was a commonly voiced question. During our meals in the dining room everyone talked about the latest war news. I had been constantly praying for the peace of Jerusalem and felt that I had "come to the Kingdom for such a time as this". My burden was similar to what I experienced during the Wycliffe summer course when I received my calling to Jerusalem. Since the establishment of the state, I had tried to keep as updated as possible on the war situation.

My hopes had been high when the truce was declared. *Perhaps I can travel to the Jewish part of Jerusalem, with the US soldiers going there,* I thought. It was not to be. Near the end of the Independence War, Jerusalem had become divided.

Together, Stanley and I often sang, "Just keep on praying...."

When it was deemed safe to do so, we climbed the cathedral's bell tower. With the beleaguered city at our feet, Stanley and I read Song of Songs together.

Suleiman Mattars, having come from Haifa, invited us to come and stay on the Mount of Olives. We had a special time there with all-night prayers. When I looked outside, I was struck by what I saw – Jerusalem's Arab side had twinkling lights, then a dark strip of no lights. Jewish Jerusalem, however, was full of light.

"Christmas in Eretz Israel!" I was overjoyed to be here. It was only ten kilometers (6.5 miles) from Jerusalem's Jaffa Gate to Bethlehem, but the s*herut,* shared taxi, had to take a long, tedious road that now skirted the Jewish part of Jerusalem. In what seemed the middle of nowhere, the driver stopped and turned around to face us. "The road isn't finished. You'll have to get out here and walk the rest of the way."

"Oh come all ye faithful... to Bethlehem!" we sang at the top of our voices while walking to the city of Jesus' birth. *Beit Lechem* – 'House of Bread'.

The region surrounding this ancient village was called *Ephrata,* or 'fruitfulness'. I drank in the beautiful panoramic view of the Wilderness of Judah.

"That's the Field of Ruth." Someone pointed to an adjacent valley. "And not far from here you'll also find the Shepherds' Fields."

The center of Bethlehem, Manger Square, was filled with pilgrims milling about. Many centuries prior, the citadel-like Church of the Nativity had been built over the cave where people believed Jesus was born. The Grotto of the Nativity had also become a candle-lit place of pilgrimage.

When we entered the Church of the Nativity where the Christmas service was held, my initial excitement was doused when I saw people worshipping a doll representing baby Jesus.

"Let's go sit over there." Stanley led me to a corner of the big, crowded hall and took out his Bible. "What do you say, shall we memorize Matthew and Luke's accounts of Jesus' first coming?"

Outside in Manger Square, Stanley and I began to talk about the "new birth" people could experience because of Jesus' coming. Soon, Arabs invited us into their homes, where we could talk about the blessed Truth in private.

During the Arab-Israeli conflict, many Arabs had fled and now there were people actually living in caves there. While Stanley and I munched on the little food we had, I couldn't help but think about the huge Christmas dinners we always had in the US. Back then, the family gorged on an abundance brought by relatives. This Christmas dinner consisted of pita bread with a little white cheese. But what joy we experienced from above, as we told WHY the Lord had come. I never forgot that first Christmas in Bethlehem – visiting cave-refugees, talking of Jesus' birth in a manger, which occurred in order to bring us to Heaven's glory.

A few days later, Stanley and I walked to the British Consulate in Jerusalem to register our wedding and sign the official forms. I stole a glance at my bridegroom's form. *He's forty-one?!* I tried to hide my shock. *I'm twenty-eight!* Thirteen years seemed an enormous difference when you were in your forties and twenties.

The church wedding took place the next day, December 27th. John Foster pastored a church in West Jerusalem, but because of the war, found himself stuck on the eastern side of the city. He officiated at the wedding service.

When the organ began to play, I walked down the aisle of the majestic church, wearing a white hat and simple dress, holding a bouquet of flowers someone had given me. I stopped in front of the altar and looked into Stanley's smiling face.

Our Wedding Day, December 27, 1949
in Jerusalem, Israel.
Mr. and Mrs. Stanley Duce.

"I'd like to present to you, Mr. and Mrs. Stanley Duce!" John Foster smiled at the congregation. Our friends from St. George's graciously provided the refreshments. Our simple wedding was richly blessed. There's only one black and white photo in memory of that joyous event.

Not far from the Damascus Gate was what people called The Place of the Skull, presumably the site of Golgotha. Nearby was The Garden Tomb or Resurrection Garden, a place where people learned about the risen Lord.

After the wedding reception, Stanley and I walked in the direction of the Damascus Gate. The Garden Tomb was situated in a narrow side street off Nablus Road. We were invited by Mr. and Mrs. May, caretakers of The Garden Tomb, to spend our honeymoon in the little cottage on the premises.

Strolling through the peaceful garden, Stanley halted. "There's the ancient winepress," he pointed out. "And over there is a large water cistern." He looked toward the nearby rocky hill. "There's Golgotha. You see the skull-like features in the rock?"

Because of the war, the rock-cut burial chamber was sand-bagged. "He is not here, for He is risen!" The sign on the door spelled victory in many ways.

Our married life couldn't have started in a better place. We called the little cottage our 'resurrection residence'.

OUR WEDDING DAY

JERUSALEM DEC.27. 1948

JERUSALEM

RESURRECTION COTTAGE

# 12

## Serving the Lord - Together

W e are planning to go to England on furlough," the Howell family wrote
us. "Would you like to stay in our apartment in Amman?"

Stanley and I saw it as an open door to minister to the Jordanians, and
accepted their invitation. Jordan's capital, located in a hilly area between desert
and the fertile Jordan Valley, was built on nineteen hills, known as *jabal*, mountain. These neighborhoods were connected by a maze of stairs.

While visiting the Brethren's meeting, we heard about a group of refugee believers that lived in one of the '*Jabal*' districts. Stanley and I decided to
join them. Our new living quarters consisted of one room and a toilet (just a
hole in the floor) we had to share with two other couples living on the same
mountain slope. Always inventive, I created a bedroom by dividing the room
with a curtain. I cooked on a primus stove. Our seat was a window ledge while
a covered trunk served as a table. The 'table' was often used for reading the
Bible and learning Hebrew. Because of his excellent knowledge of Arabic, also a
Semitic language, Stanley was able to figure out many Hebrew words by himself.

We held children's meetings at this residence. Kicking off their shoes
before entering the small room, the eager youngsters sat on the floor and listened to Bible stories that Stanley translated into Arabic. Each and every day,
we thanked the Lord for His goodness.

The Whitman family and many other friends welcomed us to their
prayer and worship services. I felt frustrated, only being able to sing the Arabic
songs by rote. There was one song I particularly loved – *Lama Yasua Yiji!* -
"When Jesus Comes".

Even though I felt rather conspicuous because of the many Arab believers present, during their free prayer times I often prayed for the Peace of

Jerusalem, including the Jewish side.

Amman was a convenient base from which to make trips. Early one morning we set out on a 110 miles (176 kilometer) journey to Damascus. Upon arrival we went to the "Street called Straight". It was here that, after having fasted three days, Saul was baptized by Ananias. Now, instead of persecuting the Jewish believers, Paul, the disciple of Yeshua, began to preach the Gospel wherever God sent him.

On our way to the Jewish district, Stanley and I wound our way through the bustling street lined with shops selling textiles, cotton, domestic articles and spices. Many Jews were coppersmiths and had developed their own unique styles and techniques. Even though their position in a Muslim country had become precarious, their masterpieces were still much sought after.

In a small synagogue, Stanley was asked to speak and read the Torah in Arabic. It was here that we met a dentist, whom we befriended. Stanley shared Jesus' words of eternal life with him. The dentist had many questions, and while his patients were in the chair, listening in on the conversation but unable to talk and refute, Stanley explained the Gospel.

My husband had a list of addresses of believers he wanted to visit. Miss Nash and Miss Stammers ran a Christian School. Orville and Mrs. Brooks, the Christian Missionary Alliance (CMA) workers, were also encouraged by our fellowship.

Orville Brooks, Ms. Nash and
Ms. Stammers in Damascus.

Roy Whitman getting a haircut from
Shukrallah on a visit to Amman.

From our Amman room with a view
of a *gabal* - mountain.

Stanley, a friend and our station wagon.

Visiting Arab refugees in Bethlehem....

and those living in Bethany.

# 13

## Spreading Eternal Light in Mesopotamia

Natalie Stevenson, whom I met upon first landing in Beirut, had invited me to come and visit them one day. So, early one morning, Stanley and I took a service taxi for the 340 miles (550 kilometer) trip to Baghdad, Iraq by way of Syria. Syria's narrow green belt was filled with plantations, olive groves and vineyards. Soon, this was taken over by the Syrian Desert.

Khan Abu Shamat was a lonely place, where grateful passengers could stretch their legs. It consisted of two yellow sandstone structures that blended with the desert sand. The driver checked the tires, brakes and engine, while a fierce looking soldier, wearing a head-cloth, asked to see our passports.

"Where are you going?" He looked at our travel documents.

"We're on our way to Baghdad, sir," Stanley told him.

"Why are you going there?"

"Visiting friends, sir." It was true, but it didn't seem wise to convey to this Muslim soldier that we also planned to share the Gospel in Iraq. The soldier waved us through.

Traveling at a speed of about forty miles an hour over flat, clay covered sand, the passengers soon became bored. To pass the time, I began to give them some English lessons and asked what certain desert posts meant, like Q1, Q2, etcetera. Not long after, the wind began to pick up. Soon, clouds of sand and dust filled the sky, becoming so dense it obscured the sun. The car crawled along its track. When visibility was reduced to almost zero, the driver stopped the car.

"We'll just have to wait for the storm to pass," he told us.

Even though all the car windows were closed, gritty dust found a way in through cracks in the door and air vents. Sand kept seeping into the car and it became stifling hot inside. Holding hands, Stanley and I began to pray.

"I think we should proceed," I said.

The other passengers didn't think that was such a good idea.

"We could end up in a meandering wadi, or lose our way completely." The driver shook his head.

"I really feel the Lord wants us to proceed." I looked at my husband. "Stanley?" Eventually, we were able to convince the driver to continue. And to everyone's amazement, we drove out of the storm.

"Thank You Lord!" I pressed Stanley's hand.

It was dark by the time we reached the last Syrian checkpoint. The desert soldiers told everyone to open their luggage for inspection.

"What's this?" The soldier held up my Hebrew Bible, the language of "those Jews".

"I have another one, want to see it?" I boldly took out my English Bible. "This Hebrew Bible is the original, and this one, the English, is a translation." I wanted them to know that the Hebrew copy was even more important to me than the English one. I smiled at the stern looking soldier. "It's translated into many languages, you know."

It was a miracle I was allowed to keep my Bibles. After many, many hours of monotonous driving, there it was - the famous river Euphrates, historically one of the most important rivers of Southwest Asia. After crossing a bridge spanning the Tigris, the taxi stopped in front of a building.

"Welcome to Baghdad, the glory of the Orient!"
The long, tiring and exciting journey had come to an end.

Nathalie & Keith Stevenson,
Baghdad, Iraq.

# 14

## A Tale of Three Cities

We finally arrived at the house of Stanley's friends, Keith and Natalie Stevenson, located near Baghdad's White Palace. Because Jewish fear of the Arabs was palpable, Aboody Dallal, a Jewish young man, began to bring his friends to the Stevensons'. Stanley and I shared the Word, and I was touched by the prayers and deep commitment of these young people. Later, Aboody invited us to his home to meet his mother, Rose.

As we were used to doing wherever we went, Stanley and I handed out Arabic tracts in Baghdad. One day we were stopped by the police. "You two come with me to the police station!" In the building, on our way to the officer's headquarters, my heart ached when we passed a 'cage' full of prisoners.

The officer took his time to study the simple tract. "Oh, I know what this is about!" He put it down. "Nothing political. I also have a New Testament. It's okay."

"Can you please put that in writing, sir?" Stanley asked. "In case we're stopped again?"

"And would it be all right if I give some of these tracts to the prisoners?" I dared to add. Indeed, we WERE permitted to give them to the prisoners!

Keith invited Stanley to join him on a mission trip to the cities of Basra and Kirkuk. Southern Basra, Iraq's main port near the Persian Gulf, had many oil wells, and some believed it was the historic location of the Garden of Eden.

Kirkuk, 156 miles (250 kilometers) north of Baghdad, was the center of Iraq's oil industry, with pipelines to Mediterranean ports.

Even though it was only May, Baghdad felt terribly hot, with temperatures already reaching about 110 $^0$ (around 40 $^0$ C). While our husbands were

56

away on their mission trip, Nathalie and I kept each other company.

"Where can I find the Jewish centers in town?" I asked the veteran missionary. "I heard there are about sixty synagogues here." I was able to visit some of them, as well as homes and humble shops.

Stanley and Steve made it safely back to Baghdad. They shared about their trip on which they had sown bountifully.

"Lord, we ask and believe that You will bring about an abundant harvest!"

The Baghdad believers wholeheartedly said "Amen!" to this prayer.

Because of its long history, Iraq was often called the Cradle of Civilization. Throughout the centuries, Iraq had been home to Muslims, Christians, Jews, Assyrians and countless others. After the fall of Jerusalem in 586 B.C., the Jews from Israel were exiled to Babylon. Here, they built new lives. In 1947, when the British Mandate of Iraq ended and the country gained independence from Britain, there were 77,000 Jews living in Baghdad. Founding member of the Arab League, Iraq joined the 1948 Arab-Israeli war. The Zionist drive for a Jewish state caused the 2,700 year old Iraqi Jewish community to suffer horrible persecution. Anti-Jewish rioting, looting of shops and confiscation of property became a regular occurrence. Zionism became a capital crime and hundreds were arrested. Many Jews fled to Basra, and from there, thousands were smuggled across the *Shatt al-Arab* sea into Iran. The Jewish Agency assisted refugees in reaching Israel.

The capture of Eilat in January of 1949 had ended the War of Independence. Because of the complexity of the situation, Israel signed four separate armistice agreements with Egypt, Syria, Lebanon and Jordan. The Arab induced war had given Israel about 50% more territory than had been allotted by the UN Partition Plan. Jordan's annexation of the West Bank was only recognized by Britain and Pakistan. During the War of Independence, an estimated 726,000 Palestinian Arabs either fled or had been expelled from Jewish held areas. Many crossed over to the Jordan River's east bank and took shelter in temporary camps, mosques, schools, towns or villages. In 1950, the *United Nations Relief and Works Agency* (UNWRA) took over from the Red Cross and began to look after the refugees. With the influx of Palestinian Arab refugees, Amman's population expanded at a dizzying pace.

# PART  4

# 1950 - 1956

# 15

## More Words of Hope and Comfort

Helping and visiting these Arab refugees left an everlasting impression upon Stanley and me. In order to reach our room or the meeting hall, we had to wind our way past little stalls selling pita bread. People even sold bread from the sidewalk. We always had to be careful not to fall over the feet of homeless people. Because there were no city maps available, I drew one myself and handed out copies to people who wanted to come to meetings.

Our days were filled with going from one tent or place of squalor to another. Stanley gave out words of hope to those who were living in dark despair. On other days we visited people living in a corner of a house, gave a little help and listened to the people's stories. One group of refugees was huddled together in a hole in the ground, encircling a small charcoal burner. I couldn't believe that people actually existed there.

Stanley and I just lived for the moment, and didn't think about political implications or possible solutions. All we wanted was to help people and bring them the Gospel. We knew God used the dire circumstances of these people to draw them to Himself.

Every country had its own problems and regardless of what governments did or decided, Jew and Arab had to personally come to know the Lord Jesus. Only then would the problem between the two peoples be truly solved.

Whenever I saw an opportunity, I'd set up my flannelgraph and share stories about God's love, using flannel pictures to illustrate the stories. Many times I told the story of "Emil in Indonesia", who found the Lord and Heaven. When there was no wall for the pictures to be placed on, Stanley's back had to do. I told the story in English, which my husband then translated into Arabic, scores and scores of times.

Dr. Lambie and his wife lived near a tuberculosis sanatorium between Bethlehem and Hebron, an area that was now part of Jordan. It was also next to the Ein Arub refugee camp where they helped out. Because he already had a car, Dr. Lambie felt that having a second car, which was a wood-framed Ford station wagon, was too extravagant. During the War of Independence, this car had been in the garage at Christ Church, in Jerusalem's Old City. Even though there had been a lot of damage to the surrounding buildings, the car didn't get a scratch on it.

"Would you be interested in buying the car?" Dr. Lambie asked his friend Stanley.

We just had just received a sizable donation from some of my friends in Virginia where I used to teach Bible. Only now I realized how far my teaching by faith was rewarded! We bought the car, which was soon put to good use. Stanley and I filled it with sacks of flour, powdered milk and other items and distributed these among the many camps and caves around Amman. We took light into the darkness, often standing in the opening of a dark cave. (One was called 'Philadelphia', which means 'brotherly love'.) Stanley handed out food, followed by words of hope to the desperate people. Eventually, our work among the refugees was honored by the Jordanian authorities. One day, I was introduced to King Abdullah's wife at the king's residence in Jericho, where they handed me a written statement about our relief work.

We learned that 4,000 refugees were living in tents in the Irbid refugee camp in northern Jordan. Stanley and I joined other workers who were handing out flour and powdered milk there. I looked at the people waiting patiently in line to receive their portions.

"There are many pregnant women here. They receive a double portion," the relief worker told me. "But we'll have to search them." I understood what she meant when it turned out that several 'pregnant' women carried pillows under their dresses.

Zarqa had been the first camp set up by the Red Cross in 1949. Located about fifteen miles, (twenty-five kilometers) northeast of Amman, near the city of Zarqa, it housed 8,000 refugees. I had taken my flannelgraph board with me on a visit to the tent city. I put it on my folding easel, and began to tell one of my many Bible stories to the eager listeners. George Kitab translated into Arabic. Everything went well until one of the listeners shouted, "Hey, missionary! What's all this?" The man walked up to the story board. "I don't want this!" he yelled as he began to tear it down.

"Please, come with me." George took the man aside and explained what we were doing. I sighed with relief when he was able to quiet things down, and we were able to finish the story.

It was a short drive from Amman to the Jericho camp at the foot of what was believed to be the Mount of Temptation. Here, in this camp, Stanley tried to help Arab believers understand the importance of the return of the Jews by showing them appropriate Bible verses. He was never judgmental, but always spoke the truth in love. "When feeling humiliated and defeated, could this be because we're not living the way we're supposed to be?" he asked them. He motioned with his hand in the direction of the tents and mud huts. "You'd feel differently if you could help the Jews return to Israel," Stanley offered. There was still hope for these hopeless refugees. God's mercy was also for them. God's grace meant that we could receive EVERYTHING for NOTHING, even when we don't deserve ANYTHING.

Costa Deir was a special friend and co-worker from Ramle who would often accompany Stanley. There, in the Jericho camp, they went from one mud hut to another, sharing the Gospel. Many refugees had become bitter and were filled with hatred toward the Jews. But there was joy in Heaven when a man gave his heart to Christ. "It's so much better to be suffering for giving out His truth, than when I used to suffer in prison for my misdeeds," a new Arab believer confided in us.

We often worked with Aroxie, the Armenian head nurse in the Jericho hospital, which was near the famous sycamore tree where Jesus met Zacheus. Children gathered outside the YMCA building, where I briefly taught Bible and gave a few English lessons. One day, after an elderly, well-educated man had accepted Jesus as his Savior, he walked up to me and pinned three poppies on my dress.

"These represent the Father, Son and Holy Spirit." He smiled at me. "Can you please come with me and teach my children?"

Badia Jahshan, who was married to a Muslim, had fled from Ramallah. She now lived in a small room in Jericho where Stanley and I often prayed with her. At that time, Ramallah, a few kilometers north of Jerusalem, had many believers and churches. Stanley and I visited a woman named Georgette, whose son also became a believer. Another Christian, Sirganian, was a Bible colporteur.

"Hallelujah, I'm walking with the King," we would sing on the way to the meeting. At a height of 2,822 ft (860 meters) the city had a commanding view of the surrounding area. Looking to the west, into Israel, we could see the lights of Tel Aviv. "He's in Tel Aviv!" Costa and I sang, "calling sheep… oh, hear Him!" And then we'd sing the same about Haifa, Jerusalem and so on.

Stanley knew the Mattar family in Nazareth. Together with this Arab family we would pray regarding present needs and were pleased they understood the Scriptures, including the prophecies about Israel. Throughout the years I stayed in contact with Ruth, who ran a pharmacy inside Jerusalem's Jaffa Gate.

In 1949, a refugee camp at El Bira had been established near Ramallah. "I feel the Lord wants me to visit the camps," Stanley told me one day. However, I felt I should stay behind in Amman, and alone in my room, I poured out my heart to God. "Lord, where are the Jews to whom You called me?" I asked. The only Jews that I knew of in Amman were locked up as prisoners of war. Like Queen Esther had done for her people, I too began to fast for three days. I waited for the Lord to "stretch out His scepter". When my "Esther Fast" was over, I was certain that God was going to grant my request. How? I didn't have a clue, but felt certain that God would use the weather toward our goal of ministering in the Jewish part of Jerusalem.

# 16

## Where God's Finger Points, His Hand Will Make a Way

In 1948, when I heard that Jerusalem had been divided between Israelis and Jordanians, I began to pray with even more fervor for the peace of Jerusalem. While staying at St. George's Hospice in what then became East Jerusalem, I happened to look toward the west. On that rainy day, suddenly the sun broke through the clouds. And yes, there it was – against the backdrop of the darkened sky appeared a complete rainbow. "I do set my **bow** in the cloud, and it shall be for a token of a covenant between Me and the earth." (Genesis 17:10)

"Thank You, Lord, for this sign of Your faithfulness!" I exclaimed, and my eyes widened when I noticed a second, complete rainbow next to the first. I clapped my hands. "Hallelujah! Lord! I take this as a promise that Jerusalem will be united again!"

It was a rainy day when I drove from Amman to Jerusalem, and I remembered that double rainbow. Upon arrival in East Jerusalem, then held by Jordan, I went immediately to the American Consulate. "I'd like to apply for a visa for West Jerusalem."

"Fill out these forms, please," I was told.

A sudden snow storm, the worst in decades, made traveling impossible. I was stuck in Jerusalem. Sloshing through the snow I repeatedly went back to the consulate, and kept asking them about the visa. There was still no answer.

"I'm going to write a letter to the Israeli authorities," I told the clerk at the consulate. I poured out my heart on paper, telling how the God of Israel had put a burning passion in my heart. Like Ruth, I didn't want to leave, but to help the 'Naomis', the Jews. To my delight, the answer came in the form of an open three day pass for West Jerusalem. Ecstatic with joy I returned to Amman where, in the meantime, Stanley had returned from ministering in Ramallah.

"You go first," he suggested, "and seek permission for me to join you."

We knew that for him, it would even be more difficult to obtain a visa. During the Mandate, the pro-Arab behavior of the British had made Israelis suspicious of all British citizens. We trusted for God to make a way.

I stored many items that were valuable to me in a trunk and gave it to a neighbor for safekeeping – never to be seen again. Then I kissed my husband good-bye and set out for the Jewish side of Jerusalem. Little did I know that it would be decades before we returned to visit Jordan's capital.

At the Ministry of Interior in West Jerusalem, a Mr. Silver leafed through my visa asking me questions, which eventually led to questions about the Bible. Knowing that behind me was a room full of impatiently waiting people, I suggested, "Perhaps we can continue this talk another time?"

The next day, I met Mr. Silver in the lobby of the YMCA where I stayed, and we continued our deep conversation about spiritual matters.

When Mr. William Hull, in charge of Zion Bookshop on Prophet Street, needed secretarial help, I saw it as a God-given opportunity. Because of his connections with the authorities, Mr. Hull was finally able to extend my initial three day permit. Now we had to find a way for Stanley to come, too.

The division of Jewish and Arab Jerusalem had not been a new thing. During the Mandate, the British had created Jewish and Arab sectors for practical reasons.

Even though Stanley and I were near each other, the cease-fire line had become a real, permanent border that now separated us. A British believer made it possible for Stanley to telephone me on a regular basis. Across barbed wire and the dragon teeth cement blocks that divided the city, we shared news and had brief prayer times over the phone. God could hear above borders! Days turned into weeks, and Stanley still wasn't able to join me. I began to fast for God to give me an answer. It was with a heavy heart that I went to see Mr. Hull. "I feel that I may have to go back." Mr. Hull immediately contacted the right person, who then pulled some strings. Through God-ordained *protectzia* Stanley received his visa for West Jerusalem (*Protectzia* is Hebrew slang, meaning that one is able to utilize personal contacts to one's advantage.)

It was a joyful day when he finally drove the station wagon carrying most of our worldly goods through Mandelbaum Gate, into West Jerusalem.

'The Scottie', as St. Andrew's Scottish Guest House was nicknamed, stood on a small hill overlooking the Hinnom Valley and Mount Zion. After the War of Independence, St. Andrew's found itself on the western side of the city. Stanley and I were now together in a room at The Scottie overlooking

Hebron Road. Little did we know it would be our home for the next six years.

I looked around the simple room on the second floor. "The sink will be our kitchen. And we can erect shelves to support our primus stove, pots and dishes." I walked to our portion of the veranda. "Look Stanley! We can put a table here. This can be an extra living room." Contentment wasn't found in having everything, but in being satisfied with what one had. I happily looked around the readied room, and then went over to the window. I held my breath. A huge cloud, looking like a big peace dove hung over Mount Zion, beyond which was the Mount of Olives in East Jerusalem.

A nation of 600,000 which had been forced to fight for its life now faced the challenge of absorbing an ever larger number of people. They came not only from war-torn Europe, but increasing anti-Semitism forced many Jews from Arab countries to flee. Most had no other place to go but Israel. Operation Magic Carpet brought the entire Yemenite Jewish community home. Then there was Operation Ezra and Nehemiah, the Aliyah of Iraqi Jews. *Aliyah* is the Hebrew word for "to go up, ascend". The Jewish term applies to the act of returning or immigrating to the Land of Israel. As there weren't enough houses for the newcomers, tens of thousands had to be housed in tents. In 1950, one tenth of Israel's population lived in tent colonies, shacks or army quarters. The ingathering of the exiles was a human revolution and in order to cope, austerity was the only option. *Tzenah,* austerity, had to ensure that the entire population received a minimum of basic commodities.

# 17

## Austerity and 'Manifested Unity'

Stanley and I began to encounter Jews we had met in Damascus and Baghdad. Like the Israelis, we learned to "make do" and lived as frugally as possible. Bananas obtained from Jordanian occupied Jericho were only for the sick. An apple was a treasure that only an elect few were able to obtain. You couldn't just go out and pick fruit from a tree – it was all rationed. Stanley and I had to be registered, and with coupons in hand, I had to stand in line for an hour or more to buy groceries. After an introduction to that process, I learned to take a folding chair when it was time for purchases.

Back in our room, I looked at a scrawny head of cabbage I had been able to secure, and gave thanks. We also received our once-a-month ration of meat and I noticed there was only a little bit of meat on the bone. "At least we have a couple of eggs a week," I reasoned, "and as much bread as we like." That was the only food that wasn't rationed. Milk was measured by the cup.

Hearing about the difficult food situation in Israel, some friends from abroad sent us care packages. Those treasures could contain a chocolate bar, powdered eggs, coffee and other items. It was such a treat, as there was no candy in shops.

"What can I send you?" my mother asked in a letter.

"Concentrated tomato paste," I wrote back. It was perfect to add a bit here and there to whatever food I was able to buy. Under the bed-couch we kept a big tray with special treats for our frequent guests. However, our desire to bless others gave guests the wrong impression that our situation wasn't so bad after all.

When the country had to tighten its belt even further, clothing, footwear and textiles were also rationed. In October that year, due to the shortage of milk, it was only distributed to children. When we needed to buy an undershirt or a vest, I had to save up coupons for months. Entering a shop one day, I noticed that they only had carob pods for sale, reminding me of the story of the prodigal son. It was all the shop owner had.

One day I was transporting containers of butter which had been sent to be distributed. To my shock I saw a huge truck skidding right toward where I was driving. "Jesus!" I cried out instinctively. One big 'grease spot' was avoided when the truck's front wheels landed in the mud, inches from our car. The butter arrived safely at its destination.

I made friends with people who also stayed at St. Andrew's. Floride Gant-Amiel and Miss Anderson lived a floor above Stanley and me. In order to get to know Jerusalem better, Floride and I began taking various busses. En route we would talk to the people on the busses and stay put till the last stop. Then we would repeat the journey in reverse.

> More and more people began to Hebraize their names and Ulpans, or language schools, began to teach Hebrew to Israeli newcomers. President Chaim Weizmann was elected a second term. He had been the only candidate.

The end of fighting had brought an increase in tourism, with 80% of them being Americans. They arrived either by boat in Haifa, or by plane in Lydda, near Tel Aviv. They came with their eyes and hearts wide open. Many wanted to climb Mt. Zion because it was the closest they could get to Jerusalem's Old City. It was just beyond no-man's-land and Jaffa Gate, which had been closed since the 1948 war.

Because we lived at St. Andrew's, people often asked me, "What's the best way to get to Mount Zion?" Floride and I began to guide tourists up the mountain, and on the way told the people about the biblical significance of Mount Zion. Especially on Jewish holidays people flocked to the site. "Wow!" they exclaimed when they got a glimpse toward the Western Wall or of David's Tomb on Mount Zion. The Christian pilgrims were more interested in the so-called 'Upper Room', situated near David's Tomb. One day, I boldly hung a sheet from our porch on which I had written in huge letters "Yeshua".

It was in 1953 that I met a new guest staying at St. Andrew's Guesthouse. The elderly lady spoke English with a rather heavy accent. I found out she was from Holland. "I'm Corrie ten Boom," the lady introduced herself. As we started talking, I learned that Ms. ten Boom was traveling all over the globe, speaking and preaching. Now the Lord had led her to Israel.

Henny Hillyer, me,
Stanley and
Herman Newmark

At the Nazareth
Mission Hospital
with Chief Medical
Officer Dr. Bathgate
and Ted Hegre.

Teaching the
children during
meetings with
Dr. Yok and
S. Ostrovsky
in Tel Aviv.

"Would you like me to show you around?" I asked her. While taking the dear lady around Israel, I began to know the story of Corrie ten Boom's life. Her Christian-Zionist family didn't hesitate to provide a haven for their Jewish countrymen against the Nazis. This courageous woman had become the leader of about eighty resistance workers, and this group had been able to save about 800 Jews. Betrayed by an informer, Corrie and her sister had been sent to Ravensbrück concentration camp. By a miracle, Corrie was released from the camp and after WWII, God sent her back to Germany to take a message of forgiveness to her former enemies. She left a few copies of her first book, *A Prisoner and Yet,* for me to share with others.

Also staying at St. Andrew's was Daniel Zion, a new immigrant who had recently met his Messiah. As Daniel fasted, he and Stanley spent long hours reading the Tenach, or Old Testament, which Daniel knew almost by heart. He wrote beautiful songs about the Lord, and even after he moved to Tel Aviv, we always kept in touch.

The years of physical austerity were also a time of spiritual abundance. In the 1950's, the united Jerusalem believers took turns leading weekly prayer meetings. One of the speakers was Canon Jones who lived in the Talbieh neighborhood. I once house-sat for him, while he traveled abroad. Another was Eilie Havas, head of The Finnish School, where I helped in weekly children's meetings. I stayed in her room while she went abroad. One day, while the station wagon was packed with children, I felt that the car had a flat tire.
*"HaAdon boreh Shamayim vegoel Yerushalaim"* (The Lord, Creator of the heavens, redeems Jerusalem!) the children sang at the top of their voices.
"Oh Lord, if you can do **that,** You can keep this car going," I prayed. "Please, make sure that it doesn't stop. Otherwise a policeman will wonder why I have so many children in this car."
At The Finnish School on *Rehov Shivtei Yisrael* – The Tribes of Israel Street, (formerly St. Paul's Street), I was able to use my years of experience in teaching children at many programs, feasts, and summer Vacation Bible Schools (VBS's). Scores of children loved the lessons we gave along with handicraft projects which tied in nicely.

After a special move of unity in the Spirit (among Protestants and Catholics) at Thursday night meetings, 'Charismatic' services were held with different churches or groups hosting in turn. Many leaders also spoke at Sunday evening interdenominational services at the YMCA. Together with a few other believers, I often stood outside the door to invite people who were pass-

After a house meeting in Talbieh, Jerusalem.

From left to right:
Elsie Churcher, Dr. Lily
Wreshner, Stanley and me.

Participants at a conference
at St. Andrew's.
Stanley in circle.

ing by. However, when people began to ask so many questions that it turned into an open-air meeting, the welcoming committee was advised to come inside when the service began.

Stanley and I often went to the services of the Brethren, and we regularly visited the Christian and Missionary Alliance Church (CMA) where I often played the little foot-pedaled organ. We also went to Messianic meetings which were held upstairs at the YMCA building on King David Street. John Foster, (who had married us) from the Assemblies of God church, held meetings on Agron Street, and the Baptists met in a small chapel on Narkis Street. During those years, Stanley and I crossed paths with many well-known people, like Bob Lindsey, who had lost a leg when he stepped on a mine while crossing the cease-fire line on a mercy errand.

Stanley was invited to speak all over Israel. We often went to Emily and Easa's house. He was a blind brother who held meetings with Arabic believers from Ramle. I always took my flannelgraph material and held children's classes in Hebrew during meetings in Kfar Yasif, near Acre. Because the children's lessons were often held outside the building, they attracted many adults as well.

On the Sabbath, or *Shabbat*, we often drove to Tel Aviv. A medical doctor, Dr. Yok, and a Jewish believer, Solomon Ostrovsky, held meetings at Dr.Yok's clinic. Brother Ostrovsky, a preacher, was married to a woman from the Dosic family. In Jaffa's Ajami quarter he often held meetings in Arabic at the place where the Brethren assembled. While the adults listened to the Word of God inside the building, I taught the children outside.

On Saturday evenings, Stanley and I would frequent a Bible study at Haimoffs' apartment on Arlozorov Street in Ramat Gan. All of his children were trained in those meetings and later became leaders of congregations. I often played the piano at these assemblies when they moved to Jerusalem.

Eternity alone will bring back those times of 'eternal fellowship'. In years to come, I continued to believe for those blessed times of 'manifested unity', as Stanley called them. As the Word and the times made it clearer, I gained more understanding about this oneness. Nowadays, there is unity, but not well-manifested, as the Bible tells us it should be.

Friends visiting us at 'The Scottie'.

Our balcony/parlor
at St. Andrew's
Guest House.

Margaret Gwronsky and me. Mt. Zion in the background.

The London Bible Society had been printing Hebrew Bibles, but was not able to meet the growing demand.
Evangelii Press in Orebro, Sweden, was able to print 55,000 Bibles to be distributed for free in Israel.
More countries began to see the need for Hebrew Scriptures and the lack thereof in Israel.
The Million Testament Campaign, Inc., Philadelphia, USA, began to provide New Testaments in Hebrew and other languages to Jews in the Holy Land and to Jews throughout the world.

Outside Alliance Church - the Bibles that we distributed to schools and libraries throughout Israel.

From left to right:
Me, Ann Leander, Grace Kyle, Russell Stewart, Mrs. Griebenow.
At one time, Grace and Ann also lived at St. Andrew's..

# 18

## Returning the Gift

Outside the Alliance Church on *Rehov Hanevi'im* –Prophet Street, was a shed where precious literature was stored. We would gather there with others to pray before we distribute Bibles and other Christian literature. With a trunk full of God's Word, we went off – to kibbutzim, moshavim, schools and libraries. Because Stanley and I were not affiliated with any missionary society, we were asked (and allowed) to give out the Bibles.

It was ironic that most of the Jews who had worked hard for the creation of the Jewish state were unbelievers. Only a small percentage of Israeli Jews were religious – the majority were secular. The fact was that most Israelis accepted the free, complete Bibles we handed out. Some tore out the New Testament and then rebound the Old Testament. However, many were impressed to receive a Bible that had originally come from Israel – the Land of the Bible, gone out into the world, and now come back to Israel as a gift – in Hebrew. Even if they only read the Bible to learn about their historic past, God's Word was able to speak to their hearts.

"Would you like to join us in the dining room?" the kibbutzniks often asked after accepting Bibles. We enjoyed meeting new people while eating family style, and took our time to answer the many questions that usually followed.

As many Bibles were distributed to public schools, it could happen that a teacher asked me to win over a reluctant principal; sometimes it was the other way around. After a coworker or I explained what it was all about, most people accepted the Bibles. Hearts were opened, and the Word went out – from Ashdod in the south, all the way to the north. Nearly every kibbutz or settlement received a visit.

One busy day, after we had visited several schools, a sudden wave of homesickness washed over me. The longing for those schools in Virginia, where I had taught Bible with so much joy, made me feel a bit sad. *How many schools did you teach in each* **week** *in Virginia?* the Lord asked me.

"Eight, Lord."

*And how many schools did you visit* **today**? He gently asked.

My heart lifted. "Eight, Lord!"

I smiled at the school children who ran to help me carry the boxes containing the heavenly treasures. While we were walking to and fro I told them, "God will show you so much through His word. He will bless you!" The joy of being able to give these Jewish children the Word of the Lord matched the happiness I had experienced in Virginia.

In the Spring of 1953, a middle-aged couple, George T.B. Davis and his Jewish wife Rose, traveled by steamer from the USA to Haifa. When they came out of customs, Rose Davis recognized me from a previous visit to Jerusalem.

"We are so glad to welcome you!" I greeted them warmly. "The car is just outside the building."

"What an answer to prayer," George exclaimed upon seeing the sturdy Ford station wagon.

"I'm glad to drive you from place to place," I assured them.

The guests were dropped at a small pension with a million dollar view of the Mediterranean. The bright sky gave a clear view of the city below and beautiful blue waters of Haifa Bay with ships anchored there. In the distance, some sixty miles up north, we saw snowcapped Mount Hermon and the snow covered mountains of Lebanon.

A few days later, I took them to Nazareth, the city where Jesus had lived. On the way we stopped at one of the largest kibbutzim in Israel. Arriving around lunchtime, we were invited to have lunch – a wholesome but meatless meal, as meat was scarce during this time. That evening was the beginning of *Pesach*, Passover, and the women of the kibbutz were busy preparing the food and spreading white tablecloths for the evening meal. We admired the large wall paintings which were made especially for this holiday - scenes of the first Passover and the exodus from Egypt. A kibbutznik, originally from India, showed us around and told us the history of the kibbutz. George had given our young guide a copy of the Scripture booklet, and we saw him beginning to read in it.

We didn't stay for *Erev Pesach*, the beginning of the holiday, but continued toward Nazareth, reaching it in the evening. The city high up in the hills, 1,500 feet above sea level, had an almost entirely Arab population, except for a few Jewish police officers. For generations, the Arabs of Nazareth had been nominal Christians, and now a large population of Arabs lived in security, within the borders of Israel, enjoying all the rights and privileges of Jewish citi-

In 1952, Chaplain Dunlopp of California, a former missionary to the Philippines, suggested the publication of a prophetic booklet in Hebrew and English. It contained the promises given for a new covenant, a new heart and spirit as quoted in Jeremiah. Isaiah 53 painted the picture of the suffering servant in the Old Testament - a chapter that is seldom or never read in synagogues. In this booklet, many Old Testament prophecies of Messiah and their fulfillment in Jesus were given. The Gospel of Matthew was printed in full. Portions of John 3 spoke about Christ, the Word becoming flesh and of His words to Nicodemus about the need to be born again (born from above) by the Holy Spirit. This attractive English-Hebrew booklet was to be distributed for free in the land of Israel.

## OLD TESTAMENT PROPHECIES OF THE MESSIAH FULFILLED IN THE NEW TESTAMENT

I MESSIAH WAS TO BE BORN IN BETHLEHEM

OLD TESTAMENT PROPHECY:
But thou, Bethlehem Ephratah, though thou be little among the thousands of Judah, yet out of thee shall he come forth unto me that is to be ruler in Israel; whose goings forth have been from of old, from everlasting. Micah 5. 2.

NEW TESTAMENT FULFILLMENT:
See Matthew 2. 1-6; Luke 2. 1-20.

II MESSIAH WAS TO BE BORN OF A VIRGIN

OLD TESTAMENT PROPHECY:
Therefore the Lord himself shall give you a sign: Behold, a virgin shall conceive, and bear a son, and shall call his name Immanuel. Isaiah 7. 14.

NEW TESTAMENT FULFILLMENT:
See Matthew 1. 18-25; Luke 1. 26-38.

III MESSIAH WAS TO BE A PROPHET LIKE UNTO MOSES

OLD TESTAMENT PROPHECY:
The LORD thy God will raise up unto thee a Prophet from the midst of thee, of thy brethren, like unto me; unto him ye shall hearken;
I will raise them up a Prophet from among their brethren, like unto thee, and will put my words in his mouth; and he shall speak unto them all that I shall command him.

7

נבואות התנ״ך בברית החדשה
שנתמלאו במשיח

I שהמשיח יולד בבית לחם
הנבואה בתנ״ך:

ואתה בית לחם אפרתה צעיר לחיות
באלפי יהודה ממך לי יצא להיות מושל
בישראל ומוצאותיו מקדם מימי עולם:
מיכה ה׳ א׳
התמלאות בברית החדשה:
עין מתתיה ב׳ א׳ו׃ לוקה ב׳ א׳כ׃

II שהמשיח יולד מעלמה
הנבואה בתנ״ך:

לכן יתן אדני הוא לכם אות: הנה העלמה
הרה וילדת בן וקראת שמו עמנואל. ישעיה
ז׳ י״ד.
התמלאות בברית החדשה:
עין מתתיה א׳ י״חכ״ה׃ לוקה א׳ כ׳ול״ח.

III שהמשיח יהיה נביא כמשה
הנבואה בתנ״ך:

נביא מקרבך מאחיך כמני יקים לך יהוה
אלהיך, אליו תשמעון׃
נביא אקים להם מקרב אחיהם כמוך ונתתי
דברי בפיו ודבר אליהם את כל אשר אצונו׃

6

zens in the state. This was true of over 100,000 Arabs in the Jewish state. But there were no Jews whatsoever in the Arab part of Israel, which was now called The Hashemite Kingdom of Jordan.

We were warmly welcomed at a home connected to the Scottish hospital in Nazareth where we were to spend two nights. The next day I took the Davis family to visit Mary's Well, or the Well of the Virgin, which was on the street level in the midst of town. We saw Arab women balancing empty water tins - large, used Standard Oil cans on their heads. Overflowing cans were then either carried on their heads or on their shoulders, held in place with one hand. We learned that the street well was probably only a few hundred years old.

"I can show you the ancient well," said the Arab guide, who had offered his services. He led us down under a stone archway, then down under an ancient church to the stone fountain which fed the well up on the street level. As this was the only spring in the Nazareth area, it was probably here that Mary drew water with an earthen water jar. Later, a church and buildings had been constructed over and around the fountain.

"Let's continue, shall we?" I suggested.

With joy and anticipation, our little group looked forward to seeing the Sea of Galilee.

The city of Tiberias, on the southwest side of the sea, now had a population of over 35,000. We visited missionary friends there: Dr. Lily Wreshner from Switzerland, now a Jewish citizen, and British Elsie Churcher who both lived in a caravan. We also met a man from Finland, Kaarlo Syvanto, whose home was on a hill overlooking the sea. These believers had been actively distributing the Word of God throughout Israel.

We spent the night at a seaside pension in Tiberias. Brother Syvanto joined us the next morning for a trip to the Hula District, some twenty miles north of Tiberias. While driving along the highway beside the sea, we enjoyed an abundance of wild flowers along the roadside.

"There goes Ben Gurion!" Mrs. Davis suddenly exclaimed.

There he was, the white haired Prime Minister of Israel, walking and talking to a companion. They were hemmed in by an empty car and driver, a guard in front and behind them. Everyone was excited at this unexpected sight.

"Can you stop the car, Irene?"

We watched as George hurried to the Ben Gurion group. He soon returned to the car.

"Ben Gurion doesn't want to be disturbed," George explained. "But I gave the guard and one of the drivers booklets!"

"Let's turn around and drive past them again," someone suggested. As we did, we all called out lustily, "Shalom!"

Ben Gurion raised his hand in salute and smiled. After going a little distance, I turned back and we had another good look at the famous leader. Little did I know then that one day, I would meet him in his home in Sde Boker!

Mr. Dulles, the American Secretary of State, was also in Israel during this time. Ben Gurion presented him with a copy of the new *Jerusalem Bible*, the Old Testament in Hebrew that just had been published. The *Jerusalem Post* wrote about how Dulles told Ben Gurion that he toured the various Middle Eastern countries in the spirit of Paul's words: "Faith, Hope and Charity". The Prime Minister had smiled and graciously answered, "No, we do not want charity. The correct translation of the original Greek is **hope** and **love**."

Motoring along the shores of the Sea of Galilee we came to Tabga, the supposed spot where Jesus met with His disciples after His resurrection. The church here was called The Church of the Multiplication of the Loaves and Fishes, shortened to The Church of the Multiplication.

"It seems that this area is about the best fishing place on the Sea of Galilee," our Finnish brother knew. While the others went out to take a closer look at the sea, I remained in the car. Seeing a group of Jewish vacationers, I gave them several copies of the wine-red booklets. Little did I know what the result would be.

Making our way further north, Brother Syvanto pointed to a small pond on the roadside. "That's papyrus, from which they used to make the famous paper. There are only a few beds of papyri today." He got out of the car and cut several of the green stalks as a present. Further up north there were a dozen or more storks resting along the roadside. I stopped the car so George could take a picture, but the birds gracefully flew away. "Migrating from Egypt to Holland," the Finnish brother offered.

"What a difference!" George exclaimed when we reached Lake Hula. "When we were here in 1935, it was a deserted, swampy area inhabited by a few Arab families living in mud huts."

"We'd been appalled at the living conditions of these people trying to eke out a miserable living in that malaria invested area," Rose added. They admired the well-planned colonized landscape. Jews had bought the swampy land, then drained it and the long stretch of land began to blossom like a rose.

We drove back to Tiberias where we had lunch with Lily and Elsie, our friends in the caravan. Our luggage was loaded inside and atop the car, and after earnest prayer for the Lord's guidance, we set out for the journey to Jerusalem.

The pleasant drive took several hours, and thanks to the occasional shower, we saw a beautiful rainbow with part of it showing a double bow. At various places along the way we gave out Scripture booklets which were gladly received. Heading toward Jerusalem, we were blessed with a beautiful sunset. Finally, the car began to ascend the winding roads through the hills surrounding Jerusalem. With songs of thanksgiving our party entered the City of the Great King.

Darkness had fallen by the time we reached the Davises' lodgings, the American Church home of the Griebenow family. Since their coming to Israel, the Griebenows had been actively helping with the distribution of Bibles and Scripture booklets. They regularly received shipments of thousands of Hebrew Bibles that were to be placed in schools and libraries in Israel. Mr. Griebenow was pastor of the American Church in Jerusalem, and chairman of the Christian and Missionary Alliance (CMA) work in Israel. I left the Davis couple with the Griebenows and returned to my home at St. Andrew's and to Stanley.

It was still Pesach, the Jewish festival of Passover, and we had arrived in Jerusalem shortly before Resurrection Day (Easter).

"How I wish we could be at the Garden Tomb now," I sighed.
For us, it was impossible because it was on the Jordanian side. Many believers now gathered on the hill under our room and had their Easter sunrise service looking toward the east, the Mount of Olives.

"He lives!" The early morning stillness carried the song toward Mount Zion and the Hinnom Valley below.

Later I heard that George and Rose had been able to visit the Garden Tomb in East Jerusalem. Usually it was very difficult to get from New Jerusalem (held by the Jews at the time) to Arab-held Old Jerusalem. However, at Christmas and during the Passover season, restrictions eased. Tourists who had made application in advance, and had been able to secure visas, could then visit other points of interests in the Jordanian Kingdom, e.g. Bethlehem. The special visa was good for several days, after which the tourists had to return to Israel.

A few weeks later I volunteered to take the Davises to Tel Aviv and other places. The Israeli government endeavored to keep the roads in good repair, and while driving from Jerusalem to Tel Aviv, we saw groups of Jews from many lands working on the road. "Let's offer them the Word," George suggested when we came to a group of a dozen or more men. I stopped, and they began to give out the Scripture booklets to the workmen, who eagerly received them.

Printed matter was still quite scarce in Israel, and people were eager to read in the evenings when the long days had ended. Among the workers were a few Yemenite Jews, easily recognized by their dark beards, side curls and dark, suntanned faces. These Jews, who read Hebrew fluently, were always most eager to receive a copy. Even though they were extremely Orthodox, hardly anyone refused the New Testament gift.

A few miles further down the road we found a much larger group of men. Again, I stopped the car, and they got out and distributed the Scripture booklets. Upon seeing that books were being distributed, men working further down the road dropped their pick axes and shovels and came running with outstretched hands and eager faces, asking for copies. We saw this occur again and again. That very day, and also later, the demand was so great, and the men were so eager, that we were almost swamped.

"You'd better give me a stack," the foreman of a group suggested. "I'll give it to the ones who didn't receive a copy yet." The workers came from Iraq, Yemen, North Africa and other lands. We gave out copies of the 'Prophecy Edition' in Hebrew, French, Arabic, Polish, Yiddish and other languages, as some of them could not yet read Hebrew. Our hearts filled with joy at seeing the eagerness of these Jews to receive the Word of God. We continued our journey toward Tel Aviv.

While in Tel Aviv, I accompanied George on a visit to an engineering company which was responsible for supplying water to many of the colonies between Tel Aviv and Beersheva. Only a few years prior, the Beersheva District had been largely desolate and barren. Today, through the increasing supply of water, it was beginning to blossom. The prophecy of Isaiah 51:3 was being fulfilled: "For the Lord shall comfort Zion, He will comfort all her waste places, He will make her wilderness like Eden, and her desert like the Garden of the Lord."

When someone told George the source from whence Israel pumped its water all the way to the Negev, he wanted to see the place for himself. We drove to the twelve-mile-long Yarkon River which flows into the Mediterranean Sea in Tel Aviv. I parked the car near the Yarkon and George went to take a look at the large power plant built there. Suddenly, the station wagon was surrounded by a large group of young people who were on their way home after school. They were eager to receive copies of the Scripture booklets, which Rose and I handed out.

"Can we also have New Testaments?" the youngsters asked.

"Sorry, not now," I told them. "You first read the booklet, fill in the request form at the end of the booklet, and send it to the address in Jerusalem. Then we'll send you a copy in the language you prefer," I promised them.

A few days later, requests began to come in from this area, doubtless some from these eager young people.

While we drove from one place to another, we were always singing in the car. One of George's favorite hymns was "To God Be the Glory", with the refrain ending with, "O come, to the Father through Jesus the Son, and give Him the glory, great things He has done". George would always add the words: "Great things He will **do**!"

We visited an elderly Russian Jewish believer who had three adult daughters who were also believers. The mother sent word to her married daughter living in a farming community not far from there, to expect guests for the noon meal that day. Not only did we enjoy a delicious meal with REAL chicken soup, but she also blessed us with a good supply of goats' milk. It was such a treat to receive a farm-grown meal while food was rationed in Israel. Most of the time, Stanley and I only had canned or powdered milk, as the milk supply was so limited that it was chiefly for babies, young children and invalids.

It was time to say good-bye, and we continued our journey toward the seaside town of Netanya. While George took a picture of Herzliya's lovely cottages, a man approached with a tiny cart drawn by a donkey. The milkman had a cow bell in his hand, and upon his ringing, women appeared with pails or pitchers to get their supply of milk. The people of Netanya, the summer resort of the land of Israel, were also eager for the Word of God. After a few days of spreading the Word, with grateful hearts for the good things that the Lord had done, we returned to Jerusalem.

# 19

## A Time of Sowing and Reaping

This year, 1953, for the first time, copies of the Hebrew Old Testament had been printed in Israel by Jewish publishers. But Israel needed the complete Bible, the Old **and** New Testaments, so they could learn of their Redeemer, Jesus the Messiah, the Son of God.

The needs and demands for these Bibles in the schools had been so great that the first 5,000 were speedily distributed. The next order of 6,500 copies was also carefully distributed by Christian workers in Israel. Even though the Bibles contained both Old and New Testaments, the majority of school principals and directors were pleased to receive them. More Bibles had been promised, and I volunteered to take the Davises to the various schools.

Early one afternoon we prayed for God's protection for the long trip to northern Israel to visit fourteen different schools. Several hundred Bibles had been put in the back of the station wagon – a heavy load for the car that also carried adult passengers.

As usual, we distributed many Scripture booklets and New Testaments to people along the way, many of whom were road workers. One Yemenite Jew received the booklet with joy. Standing beside the road he opened it and began to intone the Hebrew words aloud. As he chanted he began to sway his body as the oriental Jews were accustomed to doing.

"Arabic!" Jews from Iraq exclaimed, wanting their own copies.

In addition to driving the car, I often acted as interpreter and talked to directors of the schools. Even though one director was orthodox, he took a large number of Bibles and scores of Scripture booklets for the pupils in his higher classes.

"I have to tell you that the booklets only have a small portion of the Old

Testament, but most of it contains texts from the New Testament," George told the man.

"Never mind," the director responded.

Two of the schools we visited were in *ma'abarot* – transit camps, that consisted of tin or aluminum huts. The school director in one *ma'abara* wanted complete Bibles for his school but was afraid of what the zealous religious Jews would think when they saw them being carried in. "Please, wrap the Bibles in bundles before you carry them from the car," he specifically requested.

In another, very large *ma'abara,* the director requested as many Scripture booklets as the Bibles he received. "The booklets will be given to the older pupils to keep," he explained.

A Christian worker from the north told us about a Bible distribution visit he had made to a kibbutz. "We have been praying to receive Bibles," the headmaster of the school told him. "On the black market we found five copies, and paid five pounds, $ 5 each."

"We have a gift of Bibles from Christian friends in America for the school," the Christian worker explained. "How many would you like to have?"

"I have 100 pupils over the age of ten," he answered. "How many copies can you afford to give me?"

The team decided to give him thirty, sufficient to supply one class with material for Bible study. When the headmaster walked to the car to get the Bibles, he exclaimed, "You're like angels of God! I never would have dreamed that we would receive a gift of Bibles, and to think it would be brought directly to our kibbutz!"

Many schools we visited begged us to send more Bibles, as there were not enough in the shops to supply their needs. From the beginning of the distribution, we carefully explained to the school directors that the Bibles were to be the property of the schools and not to be given to individuals. During the day, they were to be used to teach the children Scriptures; in the evening, students could take the Bibles home to share them with their parents. In the morning, the Bibles had to be returned to the school for daily classroom use.

At one school, an eager crowd of youth gathered around the car, making it almost impossible to leave. At another school, the librarian receiving the Bibles for the school insisted that we have supper there. We were invited to revisit them. We gave out Scripture booklets in every school we visited and praised God for His blessing upon the work.

About two weeks after the Tabga visit, the Davises received a letter from a Jewish man whom I'll call Ya'akov.

*"Dear Sirs,*

*When I was at the shore of the Sea of Galilee, during the Passover holiday, a motor car stopped for a time. A lady got out and began to distribute booklets containing the Gospel of Matthew and other Scripture portions. It was a fitting place and a fitting moment to do this, as one of my friends is a fisherman – "I will make you fishers of men…!" My comrades were very displeased at the lady's activity and did not spare hateful remarks about her. I, being the only one of them with a fair amount of knowledge of the New Testament, let them calm down and then I gave them my ideas of Christ. In the evening, I read them passages from the booklet. Where there had been hatred in the morning, there was respect in the evening. I'm a Jew, loving and knowing the Old Testament. …About eight months ago I received a copy of the New Testament and was changed…. I was able to obtain a copy in classical Greek and have been reading from it almost every evening. If the reading of the New Testament became the experience of my life, no wonder that I feel inclined to become a believer. On the other hand, if I do that openly, no doubt I would lose my job and never get another. Even though I don't have a family to take care of, I must make my living. But, if I don't do it, after hearing the voice of Christ, how can I live? It's a terrible dilemma. Is there any way out? I would be glad if you would answer this letter. I'm also agreeing to meet you.*

*Yours sincerely,*

*Ya'akov"*

So, one Friday afternoon, this young man made the long bus ride from northern Israel to visit the Davis family in Jerusalem. After dinner they talked about the things of the Lord. Ya'akov realized he was a sinner and that Jesus Christ was the son of God and had died for him on the cross. However, he was definite in his statement that he could not openly confess his faith. "Oh, I wish there was another Jewish believer in our village," he exclaimed, "a man who would stand with me in confessing Christ." While they were talking, a Messianic believer and his wife came by for a visit. They, too, shared their testimony of how they found the Lord.

On Shabbat morning, Ya'akov went with the Davis family to a Gospel service in the home of a Christian worker. He was greatly impressed with the meeting and said, "This is the first Christian meeting that I ever attended in my entire life. It's very remarkable to me to see Jewish men singing praises to Christ and offering prayer in His name."

Saturday evening, when Shabbat had ended, without having made a definite decision for Christ, Ya'akov began his long journey home, as he had to be at his work early the next morning.

When their two-month stay was drawing to a close, I volunteered to take George and Rose to Tel Aviv and from there to Haifa where they were to board their steamer a few days later. One June morning we set out for Tel Aviv, and continued to sow the good seed by stopping here and there to give out Scripture booklets to groups of men working on the road. By now the Davises had learned that it was better to ask the foreman permission first, and then give out the booklets. It always thrilled us to see the men drop their picks and shovels and come running to the car to receive their treasure.

On the road to Haifa, we took time to visit a certain immigrant camp where we knew there were a number of Jewish believers. Because one of the families was poor, the Davis family had been sending them care packages from the US for more than a year. They had never met the family personally, but had been corresponding with them.

The large camp was built on the sand and most people living here didn't have sufficient employment or finances to build a proper home. The unemployment rate in Israel was high, and added to that was the fact that the government had to care for the influx of many new immigrants who were sick and needy.

I drove into the camp of crude huts and parked the car on the sand-packed road. Mrs. Davis stayed in the car with the luggage while George and I went in search of the believers. It was impossible to locate the hut number and no one could give us information about the family. At last, a young girl knew where they lived and kindly guided us to them, quite a distance from the car. The wife was overjoyed to see us and went back to the car with us to meet Rose. Our young guide was pleased when George gave her a Hebrew New Testament. When we came near the station wagon, we couldn't believe our eyes: on both sides people stretched their hands into the open car, while pleading in various languages.

Later, Rose told us what had happened. After we left, the car had been surrounded by people talking excitingly in foreign tongues. Somehow they had found out we had a supply of Scriptures. Like hungry people begging for bread they put their hands through the four open windows of the station wagon.

Calls had gone up for Romanian and Spanish booklets, which Rose put into the outstretched hands. Turkish was in high demand, and soon both supplies of Turkish booklets and Turkish New Testaments were exhausted. She still hadn't enough. After a big Jewish man had received a Russian copy he returned asking for a French copy, for his wife.

Dark-skinned Jews from Iraq yelled for Arabic literature, and as long as

Rose was able to supply them, she kept handing them out. The demand for Turkish literature continued, and she felt sad for having to tell the people her supply was depleted.

The hunger for Turkish Scriptures was an amazing thing. When the Turkish Bible Society received the order for 1,000 Turkish New Testaments to be sent to Israel, the agent was amazed. "Jews in Turkey won't even LOOK at a New Testament," he wrote. The same was true for elderly Jews from Europe. Only a few years prior, elderly European Jewish women would spurn the offer of a New Testament. In the ma'abarot, they were thrilled to receive a copy.

When we returned to the car, George and I also began giving out literature, until we realized that the supply of Scriptures in various languages we had taken that day was exhausted. Because we still had to drive to Haifa, and wanted to get there before nightfall, George and I pushed our way into the car and I tried to drive off. However, several boys stood on the running board and clung tenaciously to the car, begging for Scriptures. It wasn't our custom to give even the booklets to small children without the consent of their parents, but, in order to prevent an accident we finally gave copies to two or three of them. The car was now moving, but one little fellow, his front teeth missing, cried loudly for a book. He refused to listen to our request to let go of the car window. He kept hanging on as we moved slowly along. Finally, after George had given him a booklet, he swung to the ground and sped away with his coveted prize.

After George and Rose had left Israel, I sent them the following letter:
*"Let me tell you about one school in particular that we visited. How grateful they were to receive the Bibles. The principal would not let me go until I had really spoken to them about salvation and given them my own testimony of how I found the Lord. They begged us to return to the school and to visit them in their homes. There were four of us in the car, helping with the distribution. Two of us went to see the head of the school and two remained in the car. In almost every place, those who remained in the car had blessed times with the children and sometimes adults who gathered around, to whom we gave New Testaments and booklets, and with whom we had personal talks about the Lord."*

A few months later, the Davis family received a letter from Ya'akov. He wrote that not long after his meeting with them, he had taken seriously ill. He had been in a hospital, evidently for weeks, and near death's door.

*"There have been but a few days when I did not read the Gospels," he wrote, "even in the hard days in the hospital, when I had to fight for every breath I took. By the grace of God, I now fully believe in a crucified and resurrected Christ. I'm still a bit weak in body, but I shall try to find a living in Haifa, Jaffa or Jerusalem. There I shall have Christian fellowship and there I shall confess joyfully. If it should please you to include me in your prayers, ask for the Lord's guidance, that I shall soon be able to confess (my faith) openly and may experience 2 Corinthians 5:17 and Acts 2:28."*

**"Therefore if any man be in Christ, he is a new creation: old things are passed away; Behold, all things are become new."**
**2 Corinthians 5:17**

**"Thou hast made known to me the ways of life; Thou shalt make me full of joy with Thy countenance."**
**Acts 2:28.**

Our faithful 'chariot', the paneled station wagon, held up until the last stack of Bibles had been distributed at Kibbutz Ma'abarot. Only then did it get a flat tire, although there had been a time when we had to be hauled out of sand dunes.

Jewish road workers receiving God's Word

# 20

## The Faithful 'Chariot'

The front seat of the station wagon had a tear in the back, which I decided to cover with heavy material. While working on it, I had an idea. "Why not make big pockets in the cloth covering the back of the seat and label each one with a different language?" I saw that there could be two rows for the many languages we encountered among many hitchhikers and new immigrants to whom we frequently gave rides. On that cloth I could add smaller pockets above, also labeled, that were suited to hold tracts. On the inside of the roof I would do the same, so I could grab a tract for someone outside. There was now also room to add the 'Prophecy Edition' of the New Testament Scripture booklets. I kept supplying the ledges in our tin garage at St. Andrew's, from which I refilled the car pockets.

Seat pockets in our station wagon, filled with Scriptures in different languages.

At the top center of the front windshield I attached scripture references in five languages – each one a different color. On a background of black oilcloth, written in Hebrew, it said, "Messiah came to save sinners".

One day, when a group of rowdy youth tried to overturn the car, I pointed to the Hebrew verse. The fact that "Messiah came to save sinners" made them back off.

In order to communicate better with the people I had come to live among, I felt the need to enroll in an Ulpan, a Hebrew language class.

*"Alef, Bet, Gimel, Dalet, Hay"* the people read from the blackboard. I felt at home among the new immigrants who studied with me.

*"Kol hakavod!* Well done, Irene!" Teacher Carmi smiled at me. "You graduated even though you haven't been in class very often."

My basic knowledge of Hebrew helped me to communicate with the new immigrants. But it was the *Sabras*, the native born Israelis, and hitchhiking soldiers who helped me to considerably improve my Hebrew. *"Shalom, shmee Irene* – Hello, my name's Irene," I introduced myself to the hitchhiker who gratefully jumped into whatever space was left. *"Ech koreem lecha?* What's your name?"

If they responded with "Nahum", or "Shlomo" or any other Biblical name, I would often strike up a conversation about the relevant stories in the Bible. Generally, at first, we would chat about the day's news and their thoughts. I always tried to talk about God's prophecies for His People and their return, and if they were open, I then shared the Good News of their Messiah with them.

"Well, here we are." I slowed down and stopped at the side of the road. The open-hearted travelers found it hard to leave. When I sensed their interest, I would give them an address of local believers and meeting places near them.

"Stay close to the Lord! He will take care of you!" I told them before continuing my journey. Of course, not everyone was interested, but I would always offer them some Scriptures to take home.

"Thanks for the ride and the Scriptures." The hitchhiker grabbed his bag and, if he was a soldier, his gun, and opened the car door.

"Don't thank me," I responded in Hebrew. "You must thank the **Lord** for that. But I want to thank **you**, for teaching me Hebrew!"

Crisscrossing the whole of Israel from north to south, I always picked up hitchhikers. While we lived in Jordan, the car had transported many Arab refugees. Now it blessed hundreds of Jewish immigrants. The station wagon's three seats could hold many people on short or long trips. Some spoke Hebrew, but most of them came from so many different countries that we had to search for a common language. Many travelers asked to be dropped at the *ma'abarot* where mainly Jewish refugees from Arab countries lived.

After driving into a camp one day, we were immediately surrounded by curious onlookers. "Would you like to receive a copy of God's Word?" I began to distribute the small wine-colored Scripture booklets and other literature, only to the adults.

"*Ten li echad? LeAbba sheli.*" (Give me one, for my father). Years later, I could vividly remember the pleading voice. The little boy ran off to show the treasure to his father. I was so grateful to God that no feet were driven on when we finally were able to pull away from the crowds.

The transit camps were often villages of small shacks of tin or wood, no larger than ten to fifteen square meters each. One of the buildings could house a school, kindergarten and sometimes even a clinic. Running water was only available from central faucets, public showers were inadequate, and lavatories were often in disrepair. It was in one of these camps that I met Bianca Adler. Imprisoned by Romanian Communists, this Messianic believer had been able to escape to Israel.

As a nurse, Bianca was asked to accompany a psychiatrist while he visited new immigrant camps throughout Israel. They had to determine who had to be admitted to a mental hospital, and who could be helped to live a normal life. Bianca ended up marrying the psychiatrist, who was also a general in the Israeli army. Later, when I met Bianca again at gatherings with Jewish believers, she and I became good friends

"You have so many friends, Irene," she said. "Do you actually have enemies?"

"Oh, yes!" I laughed. "But I don't mind. I pray for them anyway."

In her book *Wayfarer in the Land,* Hannah Hurnard tells about how she distributed New Testaments. In a similar way, with our boots sinking deep in the mud, a friend and I traversed a huge camp on the outskirts of Jerusalem. News that we were distributing Bibles spread like wildfire.

"Here come missionaries!" a lady yelled. This word had a bad connotation to the Jews – the people who had given the Word to the world. *Lord, bless this woman,* I prayed, and noticed that despite the warning, many people willingly accepted God's Word, which could reveal the Messiah.

"Please, take my child!" a woman begged me. "I can't feed my child." The exiles had come home, but they felt it had not to been to a "land flowing with milk and honey".

The CMA leaders in Beersheva needed to go abroad for a short time and asked if Stanley and I would be willing to look after the headquarters and their child, which we happily did. The warm, dry city in the Negev Desert was boiling hot in summer.

At this same place, some time later, Bernice Gibson and I decided to hold a Summer Bible School. We taught from the Isaiah booklets. To my amazement, most of these youngsters were immigrants from India! I recognized God's sense of humor. "Lord, I thought You'd send me to India, to minister to the Jews there, and now You are sending them to me, here, in Israel!"

One day, a friend and I were handing out Bibles in Omer, near Beer-sheva, when two dogs came after us. It was rather frightening, but many houses had not received a copy of the Bible. *Goodness and mercy shall follow us!* This popped into my mind from Psalm 23. Goodness and mercy in Hebrew means also to 'chase' or 'persecute'. I giggled at the idea of the unusual names for the dogs and figured that if the Lord was able to close a lion's mouth, He surely would be able to stop yapping dogs. "Lord, we're continuing to bring the Good News to those who are willing to receive it!" Amazingly, those two dogs turned away!

One of the larger *ma'abarot*.

# 21

## At Home in the 'Promised Land'

Mary Wenger and I drove to Beersheva. We were asked there to organize the CMA house with tiny garden, and receive guests. We visited the main building further away, where many meetings were held. Later, I received permission to stay there for a forty-day fast. Partly, it was to undergo the experience of such a long fast (as Moses and Jesus had done), but also because of the threat of war. During this time I translated the song "The Holy City" into Hebrew (See Appendix). When I passed a falafel stand during this fast, the odor was like a meal to me.

Eventually, the 1956 war enlarged Israel and brought stability to the area. The contacts I had with new immigrants fed my spirit in His quickening presence. Later, this Beersheva center was enlarged. They added upper floors for meetings and even had a Bible bookshop. It was later named *HaMakome* – The Place! (McComb.)

Back in Jerusalem, Stanley said to me, "Don't you think it's time we pay a visit to the States and Britain?" I had never been to England before, and was curious to meet my husband's family.

"Guess your mum and sisters would also like to finally meet the man who married their Irene," Stanley said. "I know my family will be pleased to meet you at last."

The center of Israel consisted of a narrow belt - nine miles wide at its most narrow point- that was sandwiched between Jordan and the Mediterranean Sea. Because all Israeli territory was within range of Jordanian artillery, caution and stability in relationships with Arab and Muslim neighbors was very important. A series of events caused the fragile status quo to be altered rather rapidly. It was the year 1956 and it was hard to believe that we had already been in Israel for six years! There had been many happy occasions in the pressure cooker that was called *Eretz Israel,* The Land of Israel. The German government promised to pay reparations to Israel for their role during the Holocaust. Four very important Dead Sea Scrolls were salvaged and brought home to Israel. More and more *ma'abarot* closed, and people were able to buy more food and other items. However, Israelis still couldn't relax and build their country. *Fedayeen,* militants recruited from Jordanian refugee camps, kept infiltrating Israel. Their deadly terrorist attacks left many civilians and soldiers dead or wounded. In the spring of 1956 all Arab countries bordering Israel declared a high-level military alert. Was there to be another war, the people wondered.

# PART 5

# 1956 - 1960

# 22

## Visiting the Home Front

S tanley and I set out on a trip that would last more than a year. Our first stop was England to visit Stanley's family in Upminster, Essex, near London. I enjoyed rides through beautiful stretches of England. Compared to Israel everything was so green! Not only did I meet Stanley's parents, but also his sister Molly. She was a teacher, as I, and asked me to come and speak to her students.

"I hope they will catch your accent!" she said.

*Hmm,* I thought. *So I'm the one who has an accent!*

I had become aware of the differences between American English and British English and soon began to learn the way of the British – their set tea times being one of them.

Visiting my British
in-laws.
Molly on the right

We were also welcomed at the house of Mr. Bown, with whom Stanley had corresponded and regularly produced and distributed Biblical devotions.

In the US, Stanley was welcomed into the Poe family. We were given use of a small car, in which we traveled from the east coast to the west coast, sharing our Middle Eastern experiences in schools and churches. I knew many people, but Stanley also had contacts in the States. Throughout the years, he had been corresponding with students he'd met. While visiting Berkeley University, we ministered to Jewish and Arab students.

Stanley and I took turns driving all across Canada, having wonderful times with fellow believers. We visited at great length with Alan Vincent in Toronto. Stanley and I worked for a while at Haven of Grace in Florida, a residence for Jewish believers. In a nearby town I also did some substitute teaching, which helped supplement our income.

Of course we kept an open ear for news about Israel. Nasser's nationalizing of the Suez Canal and enforcement of a naval embargo for Israeli ships didn't leave Israel with a choice. The Sinai Campaign enlarged Israel's territory, but the Jewish victory triggered a persecution of Egyptian Jews. Those who were not imprisoned were deported to Israel. The situation seemed to become graver each day. Together with other believers, Stanley and I intensified our prayers for Israel and the peace of Jerusalem.

> The aim of the Sinai Campaign, also called Operation Kadesh, was to put an end to the terrorist incursions into Israel and to remove the Egyptian blockade of Eilat. On October 29, 1956, Israeli units captured the Mitla Pass near the Egyptian Suez Canal. Within 100 hours, under the leadership of then Chief of the General Staff, Moshe Dayan, the entire Sinai peninsula fell into Israeli hands.

Stanley and I took a trip to Jamaica. Stanley had been corresponding with the Jamaican Minister of Agriculture, who was also a fervent believer. This brother invited us to stay with him and take part in meetings. The island had a synagogue, at which I showed slides of Israel and spoke about our projects in the Middle East. Together with a local Jewish believer I was able to minister on many occasions.

"Oh, Stanley! The Israeli customs authorities have confiscated our station wagon!" I quickly read the rest of the letter. "They say it's because we didn't pay tax on the car." The car had been left in a Jerusalem garage for the duration of our trip abroad, and we had not known that paying tax was compulsory. The car had been commandeered to help in the war effort, but we didn't know what had happened to it. The vehicle was an important tool for our ministry, so we prayed about what to do next. God answered our prayers when a believer paid the customs tax and thus was able to save the car.

"One of us should go back," we both felt. "We must pay back the money as soon as possible."

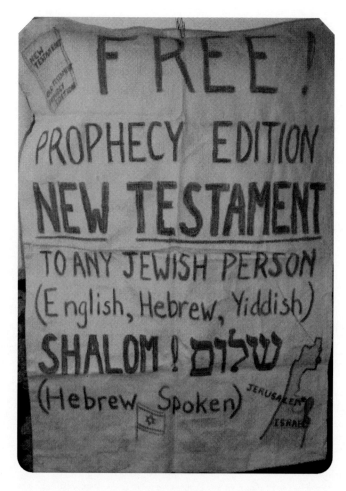

The canvas sign I made and Stanley used to hold -
I still have it!

# 23

## Secrets at 'The Scottie's' Feet

In 1957, I returned to Jerusalem where the Reid family was still in charge of St. Andrew's Guesthouse. Wanting to save money to pay Mr. Benjamin Dosic back the tax money, I didn't want to spend it to rent a room. Then I got an idea. Our car had been kept in the garage for which we didn't have to pay rent.

"Could I please sleep in the garage?" I asked Mrs. Reid, determined to live as frugally as possible. "I'll put an air mattress on the gravel floor. The car can stay outside."

During the day, I was happy to be out and sharing the Word, and only at night returned to my 'mansion'.

One evening, Mrs. Reid came to me. "Mrs. Duce!" she said. "We can't sleep in peace, knowing that you are out there, sleeping on the garage floor. We have a better idea." Mrs. Reid beckoned me to follow her up the tower above the chapel. "This room isn't in use. You can stay here for free. You know where the toilets and showers are - down through the lounge."

I had slept in many primitive situations, but to me, this tower room was 'heaven', or getting close. I thanked the Lord and the Reids for taking such good care of me.

Little did I, or anyone else at the guesthouse, know that at the foot of St. Andrew's were several well-kept secrets that only in later years would be revealed.

Early in the War of Independence, Mount Zion had fallen into Israeli hands, but the adjacent Old City had become Jordanian territory. A building near St. Andrew's served as an Israeli outpost. Its commanding view of the area made it a strategic spot. The Israeli soldiers, however, didn't have a safe way to get supplies and troops up Mount Zion, let alone evacuate their wounded. They had used a secret tunnel, but this was too narrow and had too many bends. A man named Uriel Hefetz suggested a cable car across the Hinnom Valley. "But we have to make sure the Jordanian Legion soldiers won't notice it," he warned.

Thus, every night, a 656 foot (200 meter) steel cable was stretched over the wadi, supporting a rail cart, which could carry a weight of about half a ton. The trip took only two minutes in both directions, and after supplies and goods had been sent to and fro, the cable was taken down again. Very few people knew of the secret at The Scottie's feet. That was only revealed in 1972!

St. Andrew's was perched at the top of an elevated hill. Between 1975 and 1996, at the foot of this hill, archeologists found burial caves dating from the First and Second Temple Periods. Among the many treasures therein were two thin silver tablets, rolled up like scrolls. Scholars later identified them as the priestly blessing that was probably worn around the neck as an amulet. Years later, when I heard about these finds, I was filled with wonder that we had lived so close to those secrets.

My 'heavenly' room.

In this building Stanley and I had our room.

# 24

## 'Come Over and Help Us!'

People somehow always knew about my teaching degrees and one day, I received an unusual request. "You have lots of teaching experience. Could you please give a talk on the use of visual aids at a teachers' conference in Cyprus?" I was asked.

So off I went, explaining teaching methods at the conference. In addition, in English schools on Cyprus I taught *Pilgrim's Progress* by flannelgraph, used my tabernacle charts and spoke about other subjects. On Cyprus I met precious Greek, Armenian and other foreign believers with whom I continued to correspond.

During our visit to the States, someone had given me a supply of Turkish gospel tracts. *I'm halfway to Turkey*, I thought. *Perhaps I should make a short journey there as well.* I began to seek the Lord about this idea. (This was before Turkey took over northern Cyprus.) On the sea journey to Istanbul, I had many interesting conversations with a group of friendly young Muslim men. I looked forward to making many more friends.

Istanbul, also known as Byzantium and Constantinople, was surrounded by sea on almost all sides. I didn't come as a tourist to admire the famous sites. When traveling to another country, I always tried to meet fellow believers and to share God's Truth. As I always did upon arrival in a foreign city, in Istanbul I went in search of a Bible shop, which was located on Independence Street. There, I met an Armenian believer, Vahram Tatikian. The only phrases we had in common were "Hallelujah!" and "Amen!" Despite the language barrier, we worked together to distribute Scriptures and became great friends.

I was thrilled to find Jewish believers in Istanbul and became close friends with David and Sophie Gooray and their family. I joined them when they wit-

The history of the Jews of Asia Minor goes back to the 4th century BC. At the beginning of the 19th century, the more than 100,000 Jews living in Turkey contributed immensely to the country's economic, cultural and political life.

After WWI, Mustafa Kemal Ataturk established the Republic of Turkey, with Ankara as the new capital. As a neutral country, Turkey served as a safe passage route for many Jews fleeing from Europe during WWII. Even though Turkey had been among the first countries to formally recognize the State of Israel, they had experienced a rise in anti-Semitism and anti-Zionism.

nessed to many Turkish Jews and visited synagogues with them. Sophie loved to share God's truth. One day she and I were handing out tracts when the police took Sophie to a prison. I stayed outside and prayed until she was finally released.

Of course, while being in Istanbul, I also learned about the Armenian Christians and their history. The Turkish massacre of about 80% of the Armenians had resulted in an Armenian Diaspora. People often shared their horrible experiences with me.

"We would like to invite you to our meeting," Armenian Thomas Cosmades told me one day.

After attending their meetings, I asked, "Do you think I could show the congregants my tabernacle chart?" I explained what it was all about. "I now have cloth labels in English, Hebrew and Arabic which I pin under each object."

It was a privilege that I could now share God's Word with Armenian believers as well, the chart portraying the different 'types' of Messiah. Together with brother Cosmades I took a ferry from the Asian to the European part of Istanbul. The ferry docked at the waterfront by the railway station, terminal of the famous Orient Express.

Izmir, which used to be called Smyrna, is situated 353 miles (565 km) from Turkey's capital. After Istanbul, this city was home to the country's second largest Jewish community. Together with a sister in Christ, I began to share the 'Living Bread' with Izmir's Jews.

"Rivka, would you like to come and visit our synagogue?" The name 'Irene' wasn't known to the Jews in Turkey, so I suggested they call me

En route to Turkey, with my Muslim friends on board the ship.

Sophie Gooray (right).

Armenian believers in Istanbul.

Cosmades (2nd from left); David Gooray, a Jewish believer (right).

'Rivkah'. (I always said that if I had a baby girl, I would like to call her Rebekah – *Rivkah*.)

I treasured my personal Turkish New Testament, a gift from a friend. As I didn't see any Bibles in the shops, wherever I went I carried my copy for people to see, underlining the fact that I was free to carry it around.

By train I traveled to Ankara, the capital and second largest city of Turkey. Even though I only had little time, I was able to find believers. Because I didn't want to spend money on a hotel, I took the night train back to Istanbul. The typical early morning fog hung low over the city when I stepped out onto the platform. Near the exit, a policeman was checking papers. "Where have you been?"

"In Ankara."

"Why didn't you register last night?" the policeman barked. "Don't you know that tourists must register each night?" After I explained what had happened, the policeman waved me through.

After a few months of traveling, I knew it was time to return to Stanley who by now had also returned to Israel. At Istanbul's harbor, while mingling with immigrant Jews waiting to board a ship to Haifa, I noticed a sign, 'US Cultural Center'. There was still time, so I decided to take a look inside. My heart fell when I noticed that the library contained hundreds of books, but the Bible wasn't among them.

"Do you have any Bibles?" I asked the librarian.

The lady shook her head. "Sorry, we don't."

With eyes brimming with tears I left the building. One of the waiting Jews noticed I was crying. "What's the matter?"

His caring attitude moved me even further. There he was, a Jew, returning to Israel, the Holy Land, comforting an American, because the US Cultural Center shunned the Bible – God's Book.

I had made many friends during my trip to Turkey. Years later, a new couple visited the Jerusalem Hebrew Assembly I attended. When I heard they were from Turkey, I asked, "Do you happen to know a Thomas Cosmades? I met him years ago in Istanbul." I looked at the man who seemed vaguely familiar.

"I'm that man!" The Turkish believer and his wife gave me some Bible tracts.

I turned it over to see if I recognized the contact address. Overjoyed, I looked at my brother in Christ. "You are the man with whom I ministered back then!"

# 25

## A Different Calling

In Haifa, a British couple sold to Leon Rosenberg's organization a home overlooking the Mediterranean Sea. In memory of the Jewish children who had lost their lives in the Holocaust, Leon's group established a haven for children who needed a home. While living and ministering in Jerusalem, the Kofsman family oversaw this home, known as *Bethel* - House of God. I knew the couple from Jerusalem.

"Would you be willing to help out with a children's Summer Bible School in Haifa?" they asked me one day.

Bethel's children attended either Israeli or Catholic schools, but the leadership felt it would be good to have a Bible-based school on the premises. Knowing that I had a Masters Degree in Administration of Education, they invited me to one of their meetings.

"Irene, would you like to become the principal of our future school?"
I loved children and had missed interaction with students. I gladly accepted.

The city of Haifa has an interesting history. It saw the power struggle between Elijah's God and the prophets of Baal, which happened on Mount Carmel.

In the 1900's, British control ushered in Haifa's 'Golden Age'. Thanks to Jewish funds, Jew and Arab worked side by side to build the Haifa port and an oil refinery, the oil coming from Iraq. During WWII, Haifa was the main port through which Jewish immigrants entered the country.

In 1948, when the Haganah seized control of Haifa, the majority of resident Arabs stayed in the city. Thousands of *olim*, new immigrants, found a new home in the abandoned Arab Muslim neighborhoods. Haifa, the 'city of the future', was proud of her Carmelite cable car, the new Central Egged Bus station and of course, Haifa University and Kiryat HaTechnion – the Israel Institute of Technology.

# PART 6

# 1960 - 1967

# 26

## The School on Mount Carmel

It was the year 1960. I was happy to know that a family named Birnbaum, with whom I had worked in New York City, had moved to Israel and were living in Haifa. The elderly couple lived in a house next door to Bethel on Gefen Street. The Birnbaums' house was later purchased by Rosenberg's group of believers. The upper floor of that house was to become the future Carmel School.

Andrew and Ione Lyall, together with Nathan Sharff made it possible to finance the school and buy needed classroom equipment. In the meantime, a qualified Israeli teacher and I worked on curriculum. Israeli text books were purchased along with books that were shipped from America. When all governmental requirements had been met, the Carmel School was opened.

Stanley and I had a room near the school's entrance, off the street. While I was busy with my responsibilities as the school's principal, Stanley worked on the school's account books, even though this wasn't his actual calling. My husband's heart and ministry were to share God's Word.

Eventually, Stanley went on a worldwide ministry trip, alone. We agreed that I should stay home with 'the children', the children of Israel in the school. While he was away, we kept in touch by mail. Thankfully, he was able to come home on a regular basis. Stanley and I had gone to England to visit his family, and were grateful that upon our return to Israel, Stanley had received a visa for Israel. Thanks to Mr. Birnbaum's connections, and because I was the headmaster of the Carmel School, I didn't have visa problems.

School days had a set schedule and rhythm – they opened with songs and prayer. In the mornings, Israeli teachers taught the national curriculum in Hebrew. After the lunch break in the other house, the rest of the school day was used for the English program. The children wrote letters to their American sup-

The Carmel School entrance, our car,
and Mediterranean Sea in the background.

Heidie Hardegg and I present the school schedule. J.Atmon,
Amikam Tavor (with glasses). The other name I can't remember.

Morning
devotions on
the porch.
Mr. Birnbaum
(standing left).
In front of the
window, Ione
Lyall.

porters, in which they told about Israel, the school, its blessings and its needs. They loved to welcome visitors from abroad who often spoke at devotions. I was thrilled when Corrie ten Boom came to visit the school. She was in Israel for three months to show "The Hiding Place", a movie about her life in Holland during WWII.

Because it was a boarding school, our children were free to visit their parents (if they had them) on Shabbat. Sundays were for educational school trips. During the hot summer months, the Daily Vacation Bible School (D.V.B.S.) was a fun time filled with Bible lessons and crafts, games and cooling off in the swimming pool we had in the garden. When the neighborhood heard that the program was open to their children as well, parents began to bring their offspring. It gave families a break during the long, two-month school holiday.

Parents and friends were often invited to celebrate the Jewish (Biblical) feasts with the children at the school. Plays were also composed and performed before an audience who would sit behind sliding doors.

One of these programs included a poem I wrote about Chanukah and Christmas, showing what these holidays share in common. (See Appendix). I still give out copies of the poem to my Hebrew students and to others.

Music was an important part of the curriculum. Every Thursday, Arieh Haimoff, a music teacher from Tel Aviv, taught the children how to play different instruments. The children were thrilled to have a genuine Sabra believer teaching them. They also loved it when Amikam Tavor, another Jewish believer, began to teach in his excellent Hebrew and share his artistic gifts with us.

One day, Amikam had received an invitation from one of our teachers to visit a Hebrew assembly. After the meeting, he was invited for supper with the Zeidan family, and it was here that he came to faith in Yeshua. Frieda Zeidan was a Jewish believer, originally from Germany. In Haifa she met and married an Arab believer. During the War of Independence, the family moved to Lebanon, in order for her husband to get treatment for an illness. Before Stanley and I were married, we used to take a bus to visit them in Lebanon. When Frieda's husband died, Edward Kogut, her brother, was able to arrange for her to return to Israel. Stanley and I often visited her in Atlit. All of her grown children, David, John and Miriam, are serving God.

We praised God when Amikam's parents eventually became reconciled with his new goal in life, that of following in Yeshua's footsteps, and serving the fellowship he had joined.

After school, the children were free to play until the evening meal. After that Olga, who oversaw the domestic component of Bethel, was with the chil-

Class time and playtime for our children.

Nadia, the Rumanian teacher, with the smaller children of the school.

Stanley at home in between his many mission trips abroad.

dren who sat on the floor or on couches to listen to a short message, arranged by Mr. Birnbaum. Amikam had already composed many songs and bedtime messages, glorifying God, which were well received by young and old. After prayers it was time for bed - girls upstairs, boys downstairs.

Mr. Birnbaum, a retired professor from Chicago's Moody Bible Institute, thought it was wrong that Jewish believers had to go abroad to attend Bible College. Seeing the need, he established a local Bible school. Talented Messianic believers from Israel took turns teaching the teachers of our school, interspersed with their own teaching schedules. Every morning, the doors to our classrooms were opened to three generations in order to sing, pray and start the day together. The Bible school was located on the big front porch where general assemblies were held, overlooking the Mediterranean Sea. The singing was accompanied by a piano.

Together with my colleagues at the school, I loved to organize and participate in school trips. When studies were related to nature, geography and history, the information was more easily learned by traveling and hiking through nature and the land. Meeting believers and visiting Jewish and Arab assemblies enriched the children's spiritual lives.

"Today you're going to write about what you have learned on the trip" was the first assignment after a field trip. "And, when you're done, we'll have the latest pictures for you to add to your photo albums."

Art projects were also part of the school's curriculum. A kiln, operated by a local potter, produced gift items or pieces which were displayed at the school's entrance.

The old wooden station wagon which Stanley and I had been able to buy back from the Haimoffs after our trip abroad, served the school well. This time however, the pockets behind the seats held the lunch, bathing-suit and personal items of each child. Our faithful 'chariot' eventually had to make way for a new Greenbrier sports-wagon, imported from the States. Like the previous car, it was used for the same purposes, and more!

I sat behind the wheel, one of the teachers next to me, and eight children filled the two rows of seats behind us.

"Lord, we pray for Your protection today." I turned to look at the excited faces of my beloved students who had become like my own children. "Ready? So let's go!"

Bethel and Carmel School attendees began to sing an ever expanding repertoire of Hebrew and English songs, many of which I had composed. They

## THE BETHEL SONG

Dear home, dear memory stone, my Bethel,
It seems, my dreams, bring back so well,
God's ladder with his angels I saw there,
still I see,
And each one brings me nearer
O Jacob's God to Thee;
For He, Christ Jesus is God's ladder
From earth to dwell in heaven, Beit El!

[We, his 'messengers' upstairs and down here.]

## THE CARMEL SCHOOL SONG

How sweet to eat your fruit, dear Carmel
God's vine is mine, in Him I dwell
On Carmel fell God's fire,
Elijah's God still lives,
My heart he does inspire
And oh, what truth He gives,
For He Christ Jesus is God's altar,
His fire, His truth, his fruit – Kerem-El.

The English and Hebrew words and music of these songs were written by me. 'Carmel' or 'Kerem' means: Vineyard of God. God's fire of Truth fell on Mt. Carmel, and the children in our school, located on Vine Street, learned about God's truth. These were the 'Alma Mater' songs for the pupils, who sang them in Hebrew.

sang them at home, at school and along the way.

During one of the long outings, from Metulla to Eilat in one day, I began to feel sleepy, so I stopped the car and turned around to face the children. "All right, you all!" I commanded. "Give me five minutes of complete silence! *Sheket!*"

The children complied. After my cat-nap, I felt refreshed and we continued on our way. Because the school couldn't afford to pay for sleepovers at a hotel or even a youth hostel, our little group was grateful to accept whatever was offered to us and make our contribution. It was a double blessing if we could stay at the house of a Jewish believer that we knew.

Showing Lillian Williams my favorite view -
from Poryah toward the Jordan Valley.

It was April of 1961, the same month that Israel celebrated its Bar Mitzvah – thirteen years of independence, that the trial of Adolf Eichman began. Captured by the Mossad in Argentina, he had been brought to Israel. His trial exposed the horrors of the Holocaust and helped survivors now living in Israel to receive more understanding among the Sabras.

In June of 1964, the National Water Carrier was inaugurated. The ninety-four-mile-long pipeline that pumped water from the Sea of Galilee all the way to the Negev caused uproar in Arab countries. The Arab Summit debated about the diversion of the Jordan River's tributaries, knowing full well that Israel's main water source fed the Sea of Galilee. The Syrians immediately sent their tractors and went to work. While keeping a wary eye on their Arab neighbors, Israelis tried to live their lives as normally as possible, hoping that threats of war would blow over. That hope was dashed when in 1967 Egypt, Jordan, Syria and Iraq signed military alliances with each other. Then, Egypt closed the Strait of Tiran to Israeli shipping and told the UN troops that were stationed in the Gaza Strip to get out. The enemies of the Jews were still determined to annihilate the Apple of God's Eye. The young nation had to prepare and brace itself to fight another war.

Believers from the Bethesda Fellowship in Haifa.

1. Heidi Hardegg. 2. Br. Marinskovski. 3. Nelly Marinkovski.
4 & 5. Senya & Elna Rashilov. 6. Miriam Zeidan. 7. Rose Warner.
8. Stanley Duce. 9 & 15. Eem & Abu Hanna. 10.Frieda Zeidan.
11. Ljuba Rashilov. 12 & 13. Parents Rashilov.

# 27

## Six Days of Miracles

"Remember how the enemy has mocked you, O Lord....
Rise up, O God, and defend your cause...." Psalm 74:18

With war looming on the horizon, civilians began to stock up on food, which led to food and cash shortages. Bomb shelters were prepared and ditches dug to be used as emergency shelters. Along with most of the reservists in Israel, some teachers from Haifa's Bible College and Carmel School were called up, even in the middle of the night.

**June 5, 1967** –Refusing to listen to Israel's entreaties not to engage in war, the Jordanian king's army attacked Jerusalem from the east. Soon, the wailing of air-raid sirens prompted civilians to run to bomb shelters.

"Would you like your child to come home, or stay at Bethel?" we had to ask the parents. The only child who went home was one who had been hurt while out riding his bicycle.

For me, the war became a time of 'triple duty'. In addition to my own tasks, I had to take on extra duties of teachers who had gone off to protect their country. Like Queen Esther had done for her people, I, too, felt the need to fast. Israel's future hung in the balance –again! Whenever I could, I went to the home of Dr. Churcher who lived up the hill at the Church's Mission to the Jews (CMJ). It was a respected ministry, helping Jews who were restored to the Land. Dr. Churcher was our school's beloved medical doctor and I often went there to pray with other believers.

The US Consulate advised its citizens to leave Israel unless they had vital business to attend to. Even though the situation grew tenser each day, I didn't feel I should leave the school. Eventually, believers began to meet on the

117

school veranda for prayer, which meant cleaning up at the end of the school day.

The first day of the war had been the beginning of many miracles. Israeli pilots had destroyed the Egyptian Air Force on the ground; the Jordanian Air Force followed suit; it took only one hour, and two-thirds of the Iraqi Air Force were in shambles.

Schools were kept open, so every hour, our teachers opened the classroom doors for everyone to hear the latest news. "Haifa's oil refineries are bombed," the newsreader said. Everyone rushed to the window overlooking Haifa Bay, but from what we saw, this was not the case.

**June 6** – During the afternoon English lesson, the flannelgraph story of that day happened to be of David and Goliath. I had reached the point where David defeats Goliath, when the radio news came on. All the doors were open, so everyone heard, "Israel has turned back the enemy at the Sinai Desert and has almost reached the Suez Canal." The children's mouths fell open. "The West Bank is now in Israeli hands," the announcer continued, "including Nablus, Ramallah, Jericho and Bethlehem."

It was a time to praise and thank the Lord for so many miracles in Israel's past and present.

**June 7** – At the Carmel School, classes continued as usual, with an hourly break to listen to the latest radio announcements. I was surprised to see Mr. Ben Meir, one of the Bible school teachers, enter the building. His face beamed when he announced, "All of Jerusalem is now united under Israeli rule!"

He told us that on that very morning, Motta Gur and his paratroopers had been able to break through the Old City's Lion's Gate and liberate the Western Wall and the Temple Mount. "The Temple Mount is OURS!" Israelis would never forget Motta Gur's words coming over the radio. Shlomo Goren, the Army's Chief Rabbi, had blown the Shofar. With tears in their eyes, the weary, dust covered soldiers, for the first time in their lives, had reverently touched the ancient stones of The Wall. Many had stood with their heads bowed, reciting psalms. "If I forget thee, O Jerusalem, may my right hand lose its cunning."

The rest of the country still found it hard to believe that after nineteen long years, all of Jerusalem was back in Israeli hands! Two weeks before the war, during Israel's nineteenth Independence Day, Naomi Shemer's song had touched many hearts. Now, it could be heard everywhere, *"Yerushaliyim shel za-hav, veshel nechoshet veshel or..."*, "Jerusalem of Gold' was heard from cars, shops, and people around us singing it. When the songwriter heard that Jerusalem had been united, she immediately added another verse. The song, set in a beautiful melody, became a kind of second national anthem.

This excerpt was part of the original song:
*"The wells are dry, and the market place empty. No one visits the Temple Mount in the Old City. Through the caves in the rocks, the winds howl and no one goes down to the Dead Sea by way of Jericho."*

This was added now:
*"We've returned now to the wells, the market and the square; and the ram's horn from the Temple Mount in the Old City. And through the caves in the rocks, a thousand suns do shine. We can go once more to the Dead Sea by way of Jericho. Jerusalem of gold...."*

I was thrilled and awed, when I realized that prophecies had been fulfilled right before our eyes. Israelis walked with a new spring in their steps and contagious joy spread over the country. But the war wasn't over yet, and because of their wounded pride, the enemy fool-heartedly continued to fight. Israeli soldiers were still risking their lives up on the Golan. I continued to fast, though I had begun drinking water after three days. While reading my Bible, I was amazed how many times I came across the words *"Adonai Tzva'ot"* - The Lord of Hosts - the Armies. The prolonged fasting (with all the extra work) had weakened me. When I began to proclaim God's promises, "The Heavenly host fights alongside Israel," I felt revived. "Lord, I can feel it – You're strengthening the Israeli soldiers on the Golan!"

**June 8** –The Syrian positions on the Golan, which for so many years made life a living hell for the people in the valley below, because of their constant rocket barrages, had now been taken over by Israeli soldiers.

**June 9** – After the ceasefire with Jordan, from all over the country people rushed to Jerusalem.

**June 12** - That Saturday night, because their hall was being renovated, believers from the Bethesda fellowship were meeting on the veranda of Carmel School. During the communion service we sang a fitting hymn, about Jesus the Savior, who died on the cross. Then came the part, "'It is finished', was His cry..."

*It is finished!* A shock went through me. *The war is over!* I knew it in my heart, as if the Lord of the armies had announced it. Feeling weak from fasting, I leaned against the wall. *And I'll be able to break my fast after the meeting*, I thought. Later, I learned that the last cease fire had come into effect exactly at that hour. When Jesus cried out "It is finished." while hanging on the cross, He accomplished my salvation, as the Spirit had shown me years ago, and I had believed. That same Jesus was also the "Captain of the Hosts". Yeshua is alive today!

"We're able to travel to the Golan Heights again!" we realized. "Oh! And all the other areas Israel set free!"

It had taken six days of heavy fighting, and gradually, the magnitude of the Israeli victory dawned upon Israel and the rest of the world. The "Six Day War", as it has come to be known, surely was a miracle from beginning to end. After this war, I began to share my spiritual insight and experiences with every hitchhiking soldier I took along. "The sooner we 'see' Him, the Savior Soldier who died in our place," I felt led to tell the soldiers, "the fewer soldiers here need to die in today's armies. He's alive, the Captain of Hosts!"

"Jerusalem of Gold" during the 1967 Six Day War.
The Israeli flag proudly displayed at our school entrance.

# 28

## Shabbat's Rest and First Fruits

Just after the Six Day War, a Jewish believer named J. Atzmon, came to Carmel School and showed us the truth of Isaiah 60:22. "The least of you will become a thousand, the smallest a mighty nation. I am the LORD; in this time I will hasten it swiftly." Little Israel had become a strong nation, as the Lord had promised.

"I will hasten" - *ahishana* in Hebrew, could be two words – *shana* (year) and *achi* (nineteen). The numerical value of these letters happened to be the nineteenth year of Israel's Independence (from 1948 – 1967). Six days "in His time", in 1967, and look what had happened swiftly! Jerusalem had finally been united on June 6 and 7. Awesome! Even the newspapers spoke about the meaning of that amazing date: **6-7-'67** and that Scripture with *"ahi shana".*

It was Shavuot 1967, the Feast of Weeks, or Pentecost. In Biblical times the Israelites would present their First Fruits at the Temple in Jerusalem. At the Carmel School the children labeled each fruit in the Shavuot basket after a town that had been reunited with Israel. The grapefruit was labeled 'Jerusalem'.

That Shavuot, more than 200,000 visitors went up to Jerusalem. I took a carload of believers to Jerusalem, and joined the throngs of people going to the Western Wall.

Via a guarded route, we walked among the modern day pilgrims winding their way through the alleys of the Old City. My heart sang for the miracle of it all. There it was, the Western Wall. For many Jews it was the first time in their lives that they saw the only remnant of the Second Temple. I looked at the people around me. Standing at the so-called "Wailing Wall" they were not ashamed of the tears streaming down their faces. They were here, actually touching those ancient stones! I didn't need to touch the Wall to feel God's presence. He was there, hearing my fervent prayers for the peace of Jerusalem.

Shavuot 1967 was a momentous time, for it was the first national pilgrimage to Jerusalem since the Dispersion.

"We're so close to the Garden Tomb now," I told my friends, "we should also go there while we're in Jerusalem."

Standing in front of the empty tomb, I realized that the people I had brought with me were all believing Jews. For them, this was the first time they could be here, because Jerusalem was united. I was overjoyed for having been able to return to this beautiful Resurrection Garden. Those nineteen years had been a very long time! Many felt that the verse from Luke 21:24, "Jerusalem will be trampled on by the Gentiles until the times of the Gentiles are fulfilled", was now.

Following the Six Day War, the country entered a 'Sabbath rest'. The Arab population joined in the blessings and joy that followed. Arab farmers were now helped by modern Israeli methods, and some even celebrated the Jewish Feasts with their neighbors. Jameel Hussan, an Arab pastor from Nazareth and dear friend, borrowed my "Plan of the Ages", a big cloth chart that I had made. He spoke regularly regarding the Biblical prophecies that were being fulfilled.

While Israel rejoiced in her victories, thirteen Arab heads of state tried to find a way to recuperate from their defeat. On November 22, the UN Security Council's (infamous) Resolution 242 demanded withdrawal of Israeli forces from occupied Arab territories in order to establish a 'just and lasting peace in the Middle East'. While these talks were being held, I fasted again for three days. This time, my fervent prayer was: "Lord, let Thy people STAY!"

The Knesset voted to annex the areas that had been captured during the war. Jerusalem was to be united. Barbed wire and 'dragon's teeth' cement blocks, the barriers that had been separating the city, were removed. Finally citizens and tourists could move freely in both directions. Arabs from East Jerusalem were amazed to see the traffic lights on Jaffa Road and King George Street.

Syria found its own scapegoat: The 3,500 remaining Syrian Jews were dismissed from civil service and forbidden to travel. From now on, their ID cards carried a red stamp that said 'Jew'.

Shavuot 1967 ~ Jewish believers are now able to visit the Garden Tomb in Jerusalem. From left to right: Me, Chaya & Menachem Ben Haim, Yvette Kofman, Rose Warner, Amikam Tavor & Baruch Maoz.

Marty Murphy and the English performance of *Messiah*.
1. Esther Choresh. 2. Miriam Zeidan.
3. Marty Murphy. 4. Me. 5. Amikam Tavor.

The Baptist Village was located near Petach Tikvah, not far from Lydda airport. The previous grounds of a boarding school were now a popular place to host camps and Succoth conferences, often bringing Jews and Arabs together. It was here that Marty Murphy's group performed a few choruses of *Messiah*. Sitting in a dining hall, which doubled as the chapel for conferences, I let the beautiful music sooth my spirit. An idea began to grow.

*Those tremendous Scriptures should be sung all over Israel!* I felt God was saying. After the performance, I tried several times to seek out Marty. It took a lot of persuasion, but in the end she relented. "All right," she said. "You'll get the singers from the north of Israel to come to your school to practice. I'll gather singers from the center and train them at the village. Then we'll do the same for singers in the Jerusalem area."

The students of Haifa's Carmel School loved to listen when believers from the north came to the choir practices. They later learned to sing parts as well. The girls sang soprano , the boys the alto parts in small gatherings.

Sometimes accompanied by an Israeli orchestra, the 'Messiah Choir' sang in many kibbutzim, churches and centers. Perhaps the greatest thrill was a performance at Ein Gev, a kibbutz on the shores of the Sea of Galilee, which had a huge auditorium where Israelis came during Passover for sing-ins. Our national choir was joined by a large American choir. People came from all over Israel and the famous music center was packed. The audience first watched as James Irwin showed his film depicting his walk on the moon. I had often wished for Billy Graham to speak here at Ein Gev's auditorium, but now, instead, we were able to perform *Messiah!*

"King of Kings!" reverberated against the walls. Standing, we all sang, "He shall reign forever!" and of course, the glorious *Hallelujah Chorus!*

Israelis loved the music, even when they had to pay for a seat in the Ashkelon Theater. Before that performance, they listened to Amikam Tavor explaining at length in Hebrew the source and Scriptural structure of Händel's oratorio. If people had not bought their tickets, some might have left before the singing began!

"Why not translate the choruses into Hebrew?" I later suggested to Amikam. "Hebrew was the original language of the Scriptures anyway!" My remark was a confirmation for Amikan. "I'll cook you a chicken dinner for each finished chorus!" I promised.

The two of us worked hard on the translation of the powerful words of the choir portions and were thrilled with the result. One day, we loaned out the book with the translations. It was never seen again.

# 29

## Facing a 'Beloved' Enemy

The Carmel School and Birnbaums' Bible School continued as usual. The Birnbaums regularly welcomed believers to their apartment to study God's Word. Because the studies were mostly in Yiddish, for my sake this was often translated into Hebrew.

In the past, I had been able to organize a successful Summer Bible School in Beersheva. One day, I received another invitation from the CMA leaders: "Would you be willing to teach a children's class each Sabbath?"

I thought about it. "OK, I'll do it. It's a good opportunity to give soldiers a ride." Traveling from Haifa to Beersheva took three hours by car. It gave me plenty of time to talk about the Gospel and because it was the Sabbath, I could help many soldiers who had to go either to their base or home. It often happened that upon return to Haifa, a hitchhiker would come with me and talk further with the hospitable Birnbaums.

Mr. Birnbaum had good connections with a man high up in government circles who helped us when we needed official permits. However, when the 'beloved enemy' began to stir up trouble there was not much this contact could do. There were three schools in Israel similar to our Carmel School - in Haifa, Jerusalem and Tel Aviv. Ultra Orthodox Jews didn't like the fact that Jewish children learned from the New Testament, even though it had been written by Jews.

"We must love them, pray for them, and forgive them," I always told our children. "The Ultra Orthodox are a 'beloved' enemy, because their eyes are blinded and their hearts are hardened toward God's Messiah, but beloved through Calvary's love."

One day, the three schools were simultaneously attacked by orthodox mobs.

In Haifa, a believer working in Bethel's kitchen, saw a group of rioters running down the stairs located between the home and the school. She immediately called the police. "No, they haven't attacked yet," she remonstrated, "but will do so at any moment. You must come. NOW!"

"Why are you here?" The Orthodox Jews began to interrogate Bethel's older children at the home. I was proud and grateful to learn that, throughout the disruption, the children practiced what they had been taught – they prayed and forgave their 'enemies'. Fearing for the safety of the younger children, the school staff herded them into the Birnbaums' flat on the ground floor. It didn't take long for the rioters to push their way in.

"Say it: *Shma Yisrael!*" they demanded from the children.

Mr. Birnbaum heartily joined the rioters in reciting the prayer. Seeing the frightened faces of the children, I motioned for them to be quiet and pray. "Remember how Jesus stilled the stormy waters!" I croaked. Because of a hoarse throat, I had not been able to answer the Orthodox men's questions. Eventually, it saved me from being called up to testify at the trial that followed. During the many times several teachers and Mrs. Birnbaum were called up, those who stayed behind in the school prayed. We often read Bible portions telling of what Paul and his fellow believers had gone through.

"Why are you, a Jewess, in a Christian Mission?" the lawyer questioned Mrs. Birnbaum.

"I'm a Jew who believes in Jesus, Yeshua, our Messiah," she stated boldly.

Even though there had been many neighborhood character witnesses for us, the final ruling came as a blow to everyone – "Jewish children under the age of fourteen cannot receive instruction in, or be enrolled in a school of a 'different religion'."

This meant that most of our children had to leave the boarding home. Parents and children wept when they heard it. Bethel had been their home for so many years.

In faith, Stanley had gone on a second world mission tour and had been away for almost a year now. He had been to India, Singapore and the Philippines. Because he had suffered much pain in his right side, he had been examined in a hospital. The doctor had advised him to go straight home. Instead, Stanley went to Australia for more meetings. Probably so that it wouldn't worry me, my husband had not told me back in 1964 that he had had an operation to remove a lump in his neck. With doctors unable to remove the tumor completely, he had received cobalt ray therapy. While in Australia, he needed two operations and five weeks of radiotherapy. Then, feeling better, Stanley went to New Zealand first and from there to other nations in the Pacific. He returned to the States in July.

Even though we constantly wrote each other, I didn't know that by August my husband had ended up in a hospital in very serious condition. Therefore, I was shocked when I received the telegram. Reading the grave news, I immediately went to the Birnbaums'. "Stanley's very ill. He's undergoing radiation therapy in St. Petersburg, Florida."

Knowing I had to join my gravely ill husband, I began to transfer my responsibilities to my colleagues - Mr. Atzmon, Heidi Hardegg and others. Heidi came from a family of German Templars who had settled in Haifa many years prior. She was born in Israel, and loved by Jews and Arabs. I often prayed with this faithful neighbor.

Knowing that I had to leave for the States, our Romanian teacher at the school came to me. "Have you ever heard about Pastor Richard Wurmbrand and his wife Sabina?" Nadia asked. "Well, if you're going to Florida, try to go and hear him. They are Jewish believers who have suffered greatly under the Communist regime."

I jotted down the name and address. "I promise to try and meet Pastor Wurmbrand." *Will that ever be possible?* I wondered.

# PART 7

# 1967 - 1973

# 30

## 'Death is the Last Chapter on Time, but the First Chapter on Eternity'

After Stanley had been released from the hospital, he went to live at D&D Homes in St. Petersburg, Florida. Two ladies, Doering and Dunkelberger, had created a place where "Soldiers of the cross, old, tired, wounded warriors, could find a home in which they could come apart and rest awhile." Missionaries who came home on furlough also found there a place for rest and healing, a haven where they could prepare themselves for return to the mission fields to which God had called them.

When I joined my husband, he was confined to bed, and had to use oxygen all the time. I noticed that the dedicated staff had not only looked after Stanley, but were also prayer warriors, ministering to these missionaries staying on the premises. Stanley's physical condition came as a shock to me, especially because he needed oxygen tanks for breathing. It was a comfort to know that the Birnbaums, who also left Haifa, shared the other side of our duplex. Believers from St. Petersburg often came to visit us.

During *Pesach* (Passover), Mr. Birnbaum and I hosted a big *Seder*, a Passover service with meal, on the premises. There were also daily prayer meetings for the mission fields that were represented at D&D, and on Shabbat we prayed for Israel and the Jewish people. At D&D, we only had to pay for utilities, but Stanley and I also needed money to live on and pay medical bills. God provided by enabling me to substitute teach in a nearby school. Many people staying there were interested to learn Hebrew, and I was happy to give them free lessons.

"You know Pastor Wurmbrand is scheduled to speak in Tampa?" a friend asked me one day. "It's right across the bay."

Romanian born Richard Wurmbrand came from a Jewish family. When he and his wife Sabina became believers in Jesus as Messiah, Wurmbrand was

Me, the Birnbaum's
and our Oldsmobile.

Our duplex at D&D Homes. The Birnbaums
were on the left, we lived on the right.

Stanley holding his
writing kit.
He was often visited
by Bother Swan from
St. Petersburg, Florida.

Hosting a Seder (Passover)
meal at D&D Homes,
together with Mr. Birnbaum.

ordained as a pastor. Because he refused to keep silent about his faith in Christ, both Richard and Sabina were imprisoned several times by the Communist regime. In 1959, he was sentenced to twenty-five years' imprisonment during which time he was severely beaten and tortured. Eventually, Wurmbrand was ransomed for the sum of $ 10,000. Underground church leaders convinced him to leave Romania and become a voice for the persecuted church. Their interdenominational organization, which later became "The Voice of the Martyrs" (VOM), began to work on behalf of Christians in Communist countries. With the fall of the Iron Curtain, they expanded their support to help persecuted Christians worldwide. Wurmbrand's book, *Tortured for Christ* was released in 1967.

I knew I had to go to Wurmbrand's meeting in Tampa. He spoke of the thousands of Christians who were killed, tortured, imprisoned or harassed for their faith. I looked at the man who was bruised in body, but who was a giant in faith. The people were visibly shaken when they heard about Communist persecution of believers.

After the meeting I walked over to the Wurmbrands. "I'd like to bring you greetings from our Romanian teacher, Nadia, back in my school in Haifa."

"Oh, Nadia! How is she?" the Wurmbrands were pleasantly surprised. "She's been a little sheep in my pastoral care."

The pastor's warm response touched me deeply. "Well, she's now in Haifa, in Israel." I told them how I met the new immigrant.

"Have you seen the film " Tortured for Christ"?" Sabina asked. She then showed me a copy. It was the beginning of a precious friendship that would last a lifetime.

Word spread that I was available as a speaker, and I began to receive more and more invitations in the St. Petersburg area and from my friends at D&D. "What would You like me to speak about, Lord?" I always asked. "Wurmbrand or Israel? Or both?"

From that time on, I talked about Israel and my experiences in the Middle East and also showed Wurmbrands' movie. I spoke about the similarities – the first Christians had been thrown to the lions; now Wurmbrand and others had suffered under the hands of the Communists. In the past, Jews had been dispersed all over the world, but now were coming back to Eretz Israel. I had taken slides with me from Israel and showed the public the miracle of their return.

While living in D&D Homes, we had the use of an Oldsmobile car. When Mr. Birnbaum rode with me into town, he used to joke, "It shows that the oldsters are still mobile!"

Even though many had prayed for Stanley, God chose not to heal His servant. In the fall of 1968, Stanley's cancer had reached the terminal stage and I knew I was going to lose my husband. I often wheeled him around the compound, together with his small indispensable oxygen tank.

Because we never felt the need for a mission board, this also meant that we didn't have regular financial support. God had always supplied our needs. Stanley believed in good stewardship, and carefully recorded our income and expenses. The believers at D&D had come to know Stanley, and one day I was approached by a former missionary to China who lived there.

"I want Stanley to have my burial plot," she offered.   It was in a splendid garden. The woman, already in her nineties, smiled at me. "You know, Christ may take us home before I die!"

I felt comforted in the knowledge that not only in life, but even in death, God continued to provide for His faithful servant Stanley. At the age of sixty, Stanley Joseph Duce went home to the One Whom he had so faithfully served all of his life.

Stanley was buried with copies of the Scriptures that were his life – Greek, Hebrew, Arabic, and a small English Bible in his hand. His request was: "I would like the keynote of any memorial services to be the exaltation of the name of the Lord Jesus and rejoicing in Him! (Colossians 3:17; Philippians 4:4)

An English circular letter called "Suggestions for Prayer with Thanksgiving", which regularly published notes from Stanley, had the following news about his death:

"St. Petersburg. Our brother S.J. Duce was called Home on Thursday (20th). He was in Mound Park Hospital where he had been taken a few days previously. The sowing of the body is today (Monday) at 2 p.m. (American time). Remember our sister Mrs. Duce and his brother and sister in this land. Our brother's sufferings are over; he rests from his labors. But the need of faithful men to work for the Lord, as he did, is greater than ever. Let us pray for others to join the ranks of the laborers that are 'few'."

After being married for twenty years, I had become a widow. At age forty-eight, I had experienced multiple losses throughout my life. One of them was that Stanley and I had not been able to have children. We had been able to release this to the Lord, and knew that helping other people's children was God's choice for us.

A recent loss had been the closure of the Carmel School. Despite this, coupled with the pain of Stanley's death, I experienced an inner peace. Jesus was my hope for the future! In the days after Stanley's death, I was surrounded by many loving friends. Molly, Stanley's sister, came from England to be with me.

When people heard that Stanley had passed away, letters began to arrive from all over the world. Stanley had been a faithful correspondent who wrote in English, French and Arabic. I realized what an impact my husband had had on so many lives.

My mother, Olive, came from Ohio to be with her daughter. At the grave site, the engraved circle on the ground in that beautiful garden marked the place where the body of my precious husband lay. I felt a pang of guilt mingling with my grief. *Oh Lord, I could have been a better wife for him!* my heart cried.

God's comforting thought spoke to me, *Next time you and Stanley meet, you'll both be perfect!*

I took my mother to visit a nearby church where Pastor Drew, a man Stanley had admired, was scheduled to speak. This particular Sunday, the message was on Jerusalem.

For the last couple of weeks I had been asking God, "Where do You want me to go next?" I didn't know for sure whether I should return to Israel, and longed to receive a clear answer. I couldn't believe my ears when, at one point in the sermon, the pastor pointed straight in my direction and shouted, "God is bringing Jerusalem again to the fore!"

At that moment, I knew God had answered my prayer for guidance. He was calling me back to Jerusalem!

One of the many telegrams I received. This one reads:
*"Received cable Stanley Duce RIP with the Lord Condolence from Assembly Christian Singapore."*

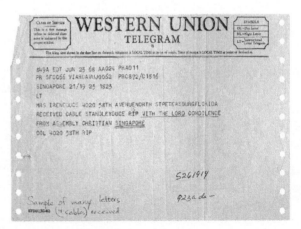

134

# 31

## Enough Light for the Next Step

I was still staying at the D&D compound when I received a letter from the Kofsman family in Jerusalem who had heard that Stanley passed away.

"Would you be willing to stay in our place while we're abroad?" they asked.

I pictured the Assemblies of God property on Agron Street where Stanley and I had often been. It had a church, Bible shop and guesthouse. Knowing the Lord wanted me to return to Jerusalem, I had been thinking to write to the Garden Tomb, to see if they needed help. But then I would work mostly with tourists.

I reread the Kofmans' letter. This invitation to work at Agron Street really touched my heart. I knew that it was God's plan for me, as it meant working with local Israelis and Jewish believers. The Lord had given me just enough light to see the next step.

Before returning to Israel, I made a short trip to Miami in east Florida. Several years prior, Stanley and I had ministered among Jewish people living there. It was an emotional trip, especially when I recognized the place where Stanley had stood holding a sign with "Free New Testaments to any Jew!" I also recalled weekly meetings at the house of a believing couple where we had taken many Jewish friends, now renewing friendships.

The Jewish people with whom I was in contact knew I had lived in Israel, and spoke Hebrew. "Would you like to teach Hebrew to a group of Jewish boys who have to prepare for their Bar Mitzvahs?" they asked me one day.

Of course I was more than happy to do so.

"But," they warned me, "you're not allowed to talk about Jesus."

"I won't, unless they bring up the subject," I replied.

Mr. Birnbaum taught me how to bring God's truth to these youngsters. "Just teach them about the four most important things in their Jewish life," he said. "Tell them about the meaning of the word 'Shem', 'Jew', 'Israel' and 'Zion'.

'Shem', semitic, *haShem* (God's Name), how important it is to carry the name of *haShem*, to be Semitic and learn Hebrew.

'Jew', Jewish – from *Yehuda* – praise. Our life should be full of praise, even as in Abraham's time, the time of the Tenakh, when they brought sacrifices for forgiveness. We too, should be thankful.

'Israel' – the Angel who wrestled with Jacob gave him a new name: 'Israel' – a prince with God, or God rules. So should our life be ruled by God.

'Zion' – *metsuyan* – excellent! *Letsayen* is Hebrew for 'to point out', so 'Zion' could mean "God's Excellence".

I often visited a Jewish couple who had moved back to the USA. They loved to speak Hebrew with me and talk about their experiences in Israel. Our mutual love for the country became the calling card, and I ended up getting into God's Truth with them.

Before returning to Israel, I wanted to give my Hebrew teaching material to my Jewish friends. "We thought you'd become Jewish," they said.

"What do you think I would need to do in order to become Jewish, seeing our mutual love of Israel and Hebrew?" I asked them.

"Just not to believe in Jesus!" they answered.

I still let them have my Hebrew teaching material!

With a new passport, I returned to Israel under my maiden name - Poe. I wasn't sure if Irene Duce's 'Christian activities' had become known, and I might run the risk of not being allowed back into the country. Also, 'Duce' didn't have a pleasant association because of Italy's role during the Second World War. However, because of my marriage to Stanley, this was how friends knew us. It could be, and often was, a bit confusing.

Even though the words 'home' and 'foreign' didn't appear in God's dictionary, coming back to Jerusalem did feel like coming home to me. I began my circular letters then, which I continued for years. I sent them to American friends and people whom Stanley had known. It was entitled 'Poe-script'.

By now it was 1969 and I had the joy of overseeing the Agron Street Bible bookshop. On the second floor was a room where a few of us gathered to study Biblical prophecies.

On February 21, I was in the shop when there was a loud explosion. At the Supersol across the street, a bomb had killed two customers and caused much damage to the supermarket. Police immediately cordoned off the street, forcing curious bystanders to watch from a distance. Many people looked in the window of the Bible shop where I had displayed a new map of united Jerusalem. Next to it was an open Bible with the text from Matthew 23, "O, Jerusalem, Jerusalem! ... How often I have longed to gather your children together, as a hen gathers her chicks under her wings..."

"Have you heard? The bomb was placed by Arab women from Ramallah!" I was told. The news made me sad, for I had often been at Elmer and Chris Josephson's home in Ramallah. After the Six Day War, Jews and Arabs had intermingled there quite congenially. At first, the Arab believers had been upset that Israel had received Samaria (the West Bank). One day, Richard Stoehr, a tour guide and friend, took a few of us on a tour of Samaria. Rose Warner, a Holocaust survivor who was with us, shared some of her experiences with the Arab believers. It changed their feelings toward Israel.

The Bible bookshop was also used for Bible study and prayer. One day a few believers gathered in the shop and watched the news on a black and white T.V. set I had brought back from the US. On June 21, 1969, Neil Armstrong, commander of Apollo 11, landed on the moon. After watching this historic event, I stepped outside the shop. *And I'm walking the streets of* **Jerusalem!** , I marveled.

Because I worked at the bookshop, I met many visitors.
"Have you ever been to Qumran?" I asked some. "It's possible to go there now. Are you interested in my taking you there?"
*Khirbet Qumran* was located on a dry plateau near the northwestern shore of the Dead Sea. The Jewish historian Josephus Flavius mentioned the ancient Essene community in Qumran. Between 1947 and 1956, nearly 900 scrolls were excavated in nearby caves, the famous "Isaiah Scroll" among them. I wanted my friends to see that 'sacred' spot, which at that time was open for everyone. One day I took home an ancient jar from the excavation site at Qumran.
*Ein Fashka* is a green oasis tucked between brown barren hills, white sandstone and the Dead Sea. Pools filled with natural spring water are surrounded by meters-high reed, called *suf*. It was always fun to see the reactions of tourists when they realized you could only float in the Dead Sea. We watched a group of Israeli soldiers relaxing in the salt water, and then rushing to the nearby spring to rinse off.
"We often baptize new believers here at the spring," I told my friends.

Visiting Ramallah after the Six Day War:
Rose Warmer, Amikam, Richard Stoehr, Badiya Jahshan
and two Muslim Arab nieces.

My room at Agron Street in Jerusalem.

"Jews and Arabs."

Before 1967, when we wanted to visit Ein Gedi, we had to travel the long way around, via Beersheva. Now, I could take my friends directly there, via a narrow, winding road that hugged the rocky hills to our right, with the Dead Sea on our left.

For me, it became an often traveled route to Ein Gedi with special tourists. We stopped at the army camps scattered along the road, and after handing out tracts to the soldiers, we continued our journey.

It was always hot at the Dead Sea. "I know a fantastic place where we can cool off!" I then took my friends to the waterfall of David – so refreshing! Ein Gedi, too, was an oasis not far from Massada. I often drove my friends there as well. We either climbed or rode a cable car up that famous hill, so full of history, with a beautiful view of the surrounding countryside. Every time I went to that beautiful place, I remembered the many trips I had made with the children of our Haifa School. How they always enjoyed splashing in the cool waters!

# 32

## People are More Important Than Buildings!

The road to Mount Scopus, next to the Mount of Olives, ran through the Sheikh Jarrah neighborhood in East Jerusalem. The previously mixed Arab/Jewish area had the largest concentration of Muslims outside the Old City. Many of them lived in stately mansions. During the War of Independence it was here that a convoy of medical personnel, on their way to the Mount Scopus Hadassah Hospital, were massacred. Since 1948, the area had been under Jordanian control, and off-limits for Jews. That changed when it was recaptured by Israel during the Six Day War in 1967. After the war, the East Jerusalem neighborhood was favored by diplomatic missions and consulates. In the same area were the American Colony Hotel, Shepherd Hotel and St. George's Cathedral.

"There is this Jewish lady in Sheikh Jarrah," the Josephson family told me, "who will be the first to deliver her Jewish baby in East Jerusalem. Her husband is abroad, and she feels lonely. Would you mind spending some time with her?"

As often as possible, I went to the house of my new-found friend. We had wonderful times because the house was a meeting place for prominent people, Jews and Arabs. I rubbed shoulders with a Jewish military officer, Eli, and with Ali, the Arab owner of the East Holy Land Hotel. Ali also had a center near the Dead Sea, which became very popular among Jews, Arabs and tourists whom I often took there on tours.

One day I visited my Jewish friend, who by now had delivered her baby, when a neighbor came in with most upsetting news. "Someone set fire to the El Aqsa Mosque!" With El Aqsa Mosque being the third most holy site in the Moslem world, the two of us felt vulnerable, because Sheikh Jarrah, where she lived, was a mostly Muslim neighborhood.

Rumors were rife – at first Israel was held responsible, then the Americans were suspect. Stuck in the midst of angry and suspicious Arab Muslim neighbors, the two of us, one Jewish, the other American, tried to find a way to face the neighbors.

"Why are buildings so important to people?" I wondered out loud. "They are constructions by Muslims, Jews or Christians. I believe that PEOPLE are more important than structures!" We sighed with relief when the culprit was apprehended –a mentally ill Australian tourist.

Even though I was often with my East Jerusalem friend, I continued to live at the Agron Street Center. Through the bookshop, wonderful contacts opened up and I enjoyed talks with customers and friends. Besides my work there, I corresponded with Stanley's friends, who continued to miss him. I felt a burden for God's church in Jerusalem, of which I had become an integral part. Ecumenical meetings were held at the YMCA on King David Street. At our assembly we saw the need for Hebrew songs. We believers took turns holding charts with the songs' translations. Sometimes they contained newly written Hebrew songs. It was a joyful day when the Hebrew songs were bundled into a booklet. Gradually, more and more Hebrew songs were composed, and new Hebrew speaking congregations began to use them.

The War of Attrition between Egypt and Israel wasn't over yet. A new song in Israel, *Balada Lachovesh* was a ballad of a medic who gave his life while rescuing a wounded soldier. When the soldier realizes that he is alive, but the medic is dead, he cries out, *"Ahi, ahi sheli!"*, "My brother, oh, my brother!" The song illustrated God's truth so well that I placed an open Hebrew Bible in the shop window, showing Isaiah 61: "The Spirit anointed Me [Messiah] to 'bind up' the wounded." The Hebrew word for heal or bind up is the root of *Chovesh* - 'medic' in modern Hebrew. Messiah was the *Chovesh* who gave His life so that we could live – He truly was "Israel's Brother".

*Balada Lachovesh* could be heard everywhere you went – in the shops, on the street, from radios or people singing loudly *"Ahi, ahi sheli!"*

I often drove people to and from the airport. The evening that the song was aired for the first time, I was on my way back to Jerusalem, driving all alone. A new song came to me with a theme similar to Israel's 'Brother' song.

I had often spoken or written of Joseph and his brothers. "This Brother of thine, of all mankind… Behold, Who I am, God's Son and God's Lamb…"

I realized anew that the same Spirit who works in individual believers also works in Israel as a nation. In the same way God often works in Israel and in the true Biblical Church, who are both chosen.

Elhanan Ben Avraham had written a Bible study about the many ways Joseph was a prophetic picture of Jesus. I wrote to Stanley's friend Mr. Bown in England, who understood this Truth. He arranged for the study to be printed into a booklet. Later, the English version was followed by Hebrew and Russian translations. When Hebrew speaking congregations would read the weekly *Parasha,* or Scripture reading, about Joseph, copies of the booklet were given out. Interested individuals also received copies of it.

Victor Smadga, together with the Kofman and Goren families (formerly Garfinkel), shared the vision to begin meeting together, and eventually, this group became recognized as an *amutah* – a non-profit organization.

We were sad to hear the news that the owners of the Assembly of God building wanted to sell the historic spot on Agron Street. It had been a place where believers in Christ experienced so many blessings. Now all that had to come to an end.

"Can't we ask believers to persuade their supporters to buy the building?" I advocated. But God had another plan. Around the same time, an anonymous donor bought a building at 56 Prophet Street (Rehov HaNevi'im), which had been owned by the CMA. The little church had been a place for work among Arab believers, who had found a new meeting place in the Old City's Christian Quarter.

After the closure of Agron Street, the group of Jewish believers started the first Hebrew speaking, non-denominational, Jewish-led assembly at 56 Prophet Street. In years to come, many similar congregations were established throughout Israel, based on the model of Jewish congregations during New Testament times.

# OUR BROTHER ~ THE MESSIAH

A Dreamer of dreams to many He seems,
As He, o'er His brothers, grieves.
His stripes and His cloak  to envy provoke.
To Him, must they bow their sheaves?

The Father at Home, for His sons as they roam,
Behold how His loving heart yearns.
He sends forth His Son, His own chose One,
The stripes in that cloak He earns.

His cloak dipped in Blood, to the pit and then sold,
He, pieces of sliver won;
To Gentiles, the world, and prison was hurled.
Death swallowed Life's purest Son.
But down in the depths God spoke to this death
And out of its sea He was cast;
Interpreting dreams of slaves and of kings
To honor and fame at last.

All ye who would live unto this One give
Thine homage, and take thy food.
His brothers, come see that Rulers is He,
Who makes you such feasts and good.

This brother of thine, of all of mankind,
He weeps as he sees you repent
"Behold Who I am, God's Son and God's Lamb
For LIFE I before was sent.

# 33

## 'God Doesn't Demand Success or Profit, but Obedience'

I missed my work at the Agron Bible bookshop, and was happy to volunteer in another Bible shop. This one was on a busy corner, and run by the Ransom family. It was such a joy working there, and I continued to have deep conversations with the customers. But what I treasured most was being able to give Hebrew lessons and talk with Hebrew University students who would come to buy Bibles. Many were visibly touched when I showed them the connection between Joseph and Yeshua.

"Why can't you come to the university and teach there?" a student suggested.

Margaret Gavronsky was a Jewish believer from Switzerland who had become a good friend of mine. She had just bought a new apartment in Ramat Eshkol - a newly built Jerusalem neighborhood on what, until 1967, had been no-man's-land. It was near Ammunition Hill, the place where many Jewish soldiers gave their lives clearing away enemy trenches. Their sacrifices paved the way for a united Jerusalem.

"Would you like to rent one of my rooms?" Margaret asked me.

The two of us began to host many events around spiritual and Zionist themes. Most of Margaret's visitors spoke German, and after six months I felt it was time to relinquish my room to her German speaking friends.

"Jerusalem is now united," I told Margaret, "and I have a calling to keep it so. I'm going to rent an apartment in Sheikh Jarrah."

Opposite the Ambassador's Hotel on Nablus Road (in former Jordanian territory) was a large apartment for rent. When I noticed the hotel's huge Magen David overshadowing me, I just knew it was the right place. After the contract was signed, I set to work. Using green burlap, I divided the large entrance

144

hall and furnished the apartment with secondhand items bought at Jewish and Arab shops.

"I'll call it 'Abraham's Tent'," I decided, pleased with the potential. "And now, let's have some music." At random, I chose a record from a Jewish believer friend who was a former opera singer. My mouth fell open when I heard, "Bless this house, O Lord, we pray. Keep it safe by night and day."

The huge apartment had been rented in faith and the Lord sent the people- famous and not so well-known. But everyone was precious in God's eyes, so I welcomed them all in. "How much does it cost?" a newly arrived guest wanted to know.

"You can contribute what you can afford," I told them. "You can also use the phone, but for that you can pay the regular fees."

Abraham's Tent was used to host house guests as well as weekly Bible readings, which took place in the parlor. We began with the book of Genesis, from which participants would discover the Bible's Hebrew and Arabic roots. Jews and Arabs together learned about the many spiritual truths that lie hidden under seemingly everyday words. On a larger scale, believers from all kinds of denominations held gatherings on a regular basis. My heart overflowed with joy when it was my turn to host them and I found the hall filled with a mix of believers. It was a journey of faith, but the Lord always provided for my needs.

Ever since that first encounter in Florida, I felt a special bond with the Wurmbrands and was thrilled when they came to Israel. I dropped everything I was doing and drove the couple all over Israel, helping them distribute their books and films. Pastor Wurmbrand would not be lauded, only *Yeshua*, (Jesus) and I felt privileged to get a taste of the victory over 'death' they had experienced and the fact that they were willing to stay once in my 'tent'.

When I drove the Wurmbrands to visit their family, they introduced me to his brothers who lived in Tel Aviv, Haifa and Jerusalem. And of course, I took them to the places where Jesus had suffered. It very much related to those believers who, even today, were suffering for being part of His Body. A German believer filmed these places to which I took them.

I was able to arrange and cooperate in many speaking engagements for the Wurmbrands. People listened in awe as they shared about their life under Communism, and how they were tortured because of their faith in Yeshua. Large groups at the Garden Tomb listened in awe when he shared that the risen Lord had raised them, too.

The Wurmbrands organized a conference at the YMCA in East Jerusalem. Many believers, some living in Israel, who likewise had been able to escape the

Communists' clutches, attended the event. It was a time to celebrate God's goodness.

Corrie ten Boom was in the country again and it seemed the seventy-eight year old woman wasn't planning to retire soon. The previous year, Corrie had been invited by Yad Vashem to attend a ceremony in which a tree was planted in her honor on the Avenue of the Righteous Gentiles. I always loved to meet with this woman of God.

"I heard you have an Abraham's Tent," quipped Corrie, who wanted to know more about the place. "My nephew and his family are also thinking of coming to minister in Israel," Corrie said. "They're talented musicians. May I give them your address?"

"By all means, yes!" I responded. "What's his name?"

"Pieter van Woerden."

My friendship with the Wurmbrands lasted a lifetime.

# 34

## Musicians' Launching Pad

A s a teenager, Pieter van Woerden, Corrie ten Boom's favorite nephew, often played the church organ. When Nazi Germany invaded Holland, they forbade people to sing the national anthem. One day in 1942, after the eighteen-year-old played the forbidden national anthem during a church service, the Nazis sent him to prison. It was there that he became a born-again believer. After his release, Pieter became active in Corrie's resistance group. Under cover of darkness, Pieter transported many Jewish children to secret hiding places. In doing so, he saved them from the Nazis and certain death.

One day, I stood face to face with Pieter van Woerden. "Do you know a place where we can park our caravan?" he asked.

I pointed to a perfect spot in my back yard. "You can use the facilities in this apartment." I looked at the house on wheels. "Make sure to lock it."

But Pieter trusted God to protect their musical instruments and belongings, and left the trailer unlocked. He and his wife Inge had been ministering at The Garden Tomb, where in 1968 Jan Willem van der Hoeven had become caretaker. The charismatic man always preached a powerful message of the living Savior and living Israel to thousands of pilgrims visiting the Resurrection Garden. On Sunday mornings I often took visitors there, and at times played piano for the services. The Garden Tomb was a meeting place for believers from all over the world.

A handsome couple received a warm welcome in Abraham's Tent. Merv and Merla Watson were two extremely gifted musicians, who had been in full-time music ministry for several years now. Merla wrote the music she and her husband sang and played, accompanied by different instruments and dressed in colorful Israeli costumes. As their ministry was also faith-based, they met the van Woerden family in the 'tent'.

When the van Woerdens were invited to sing at kibbutz Kiryat HaNevi'im, I took the Watsons along. This resulted in an invitation for them to sing there as well. The opposite also happened – when the Watsons were invited, the van Woerdens followed.

Pieter van Woerden arranged a huge gathering with Jewish and Arab believers on the Mount of Olives. It was a joyful time of ministering but it was also strenuous.

I was shocked to hear that Pieter had been rushed to Hadassah Hospital because of a massive heart attack. The doctor on call skillfully saved Pieter's life, and when he began to recuperate, Pieter thanked the medical staff for their care. He found out that the doctor had immigrated to Israel from Holland, and they began talking about where they had lived during the Second World War. Suddenly, both doctor and patient burst into tears as they realized that the doctor had been one of the Jewish children Pieter had rescued. And now, God had enabled this doctor to save Pieter's life.

Art Katz and Paul Gordon were American Messianic believers who wanted to make Aliyah. While living in Karmiel, they were asked by an Orthodox Jewish man for an autographed Bible. Of course they were more than happy to give him one and prayed God would open the man's eyes to the Truth. The two friends were shocked to find out that the Orthodox Jew belonged to the anti-missionary society *Yad l'Achim*. Accused of missionary activities, the two believers came to Sheikh Jarrah's 'tent of refuge'.

I encouraged my brothers in Christ and their families and began to teach them Hebrew. We often talked and prayed about God's ministry and His body in Israel.

# 35

## *Shalom-Salaam!* and Working Toward Peace

Anita Kiekhaefer, an experienced film maker from America, came to stay with me for a while. She and I decided to make a film about Jewish-Arab relations. *Shalom-Salaam* we called the production for which we both wrote the script. The film was a 28 ½ minute colored documentary using a film story of peace and wonder in Jerusalem since the Six Day War. It was to be a time capsule of up-to-date materials on peace developments between Arabs and Jews. Following is an excerpt of a circular letter in which I explained what the movie was about.

"Jerusalem, the city of peace, is bursting from within, from its birth pangs of the past into new life and meaning, into that peace for which generations untold, and for which many throughout the world, especially Bible lovers, have been praying. The world renowned figure of Abraham as the Father of Faith and, as the world would say, of the three monotheistic religions, is also perpetuated in his two sons, Isaac and Ishmael. Through their being brought to peace, especially in this famous city of peace, the whole world will be blessed. Children, the hope of the future, in each group separately and in their intermingling, are bringing to light that new fulfillment for which Jewish and Arab peoples, and all men of good will, await.

Not only do we see the Jewish people returning according to prophecy, forming a people out of the graveyards of exile and holocaust, proving that the God of the Bible lives, but we also see the resulting fulfillment in physical and cultural restoration of the country. It is evidenced everywhere in the land, but it is particularly revealed more recently in Jerusalem, back under the seed of David, as foretold. Above all this, the most recent of wonders is the spiritual fulfillment and understandings in the down-to-earth business of learning to ex-

149

perience peace with an historical and potential enemy. It is evident in shopping and business encounters, in sharing by dialogue, in clubs, home exchange visits and various meetings.

The film itself is a story about Jerusalem and the peace between Jews and Arabs. The film entitled *Shalom-Salaam* is an account of the prophetic and miraculous rebuilding of Jerusalem and move toward social and spiritual unity since the Six Day War. Much of the film story is based on God's promises to both Semitic peoples who are part of the First Covenant of Abraham.

We cut back to the Passover and the lighted menorah behind which the children are seated. The children take the candles and pass them to each other. We dissolve to other scenes of Jewish children lighting candles taken from the Chanukiah, to another scene of an Arab child lighting a lamp or torch which lights the way of a darkened path. Interspersed with other pictures of children and light, we conclude with Jewish and Arabic children, in turn, passing on the lighted candles to the audience. This is accompanied by a peace song and words of Scripture."

I knew a Jewish believer who taught English in a school in Savyon, near Tel Aviv. We had often talked about bringing Jewish and Arab school children together in their common denominator of the Old Testament.

"Wouldn't it be great to have a 'Passover' in our house?" I suggested. The teacher thought it was a wonderful idea. "But what about our house?" I suddenly realized. "It isn't exactly *kosher l'Pesach.*" (Kosher for Passover, no yeast products in the house.)

"Don't worry," the teacher said. "Pesach is still a few weeks away."

Accompanied by several mothers, the teacher took her class to Jerusalem. Before the program began, Jewish children from Savyon played in the garden with Arab children from The Finnish School in Jerusalem. It was marvelous to see how they communicated with each other. Then everyone was invited to come and sit around the big table. "We're going to read parts of the Passover *Hagadah* in Hebrew and English. Those parts are in our Bible," I explained. "And of course, we're going to sing many beautiful songs."

The joint Pesach celebration left a deep impression on all who attended - adults and children alike. Anita incorporated it in the *Shalom-Salaam* documentary, along with shots from Leonardo da Vinci's painting, "The Last Supper", of which we had a print hanging on the wall.

Anita often stayed at the City Hotel across from where I lived. One day she noticed a large group of Mormons were staying there.

"Let's invite them over to my big hall," I suggested. "We can show them Billy Graham's movie." "His Land" was a professional movie that showed the up-to-date fulfillment of prophecy.

The musical documentary celebrated the land of Israel, and explained the country's history through information and song. Cliff Barrows, the narrator, studied the Old Testament prophecies, while Cliff Richard sang songs, mainly composed by Ralph Carmichael, about them. The film included a trip to Bethlehem, Nazareth, and the Galilee as well as a look at the life of Jesus, and concluded with an appeal for salvation. Cliff Barrows used to work together with evangelist Billy Graham, who sponsored the production.

I was privileged to be able to show this excellent film often, using a movie projector from our Haifa school.

"This is how Christians see Biblical prophecies being fulfilled," I always told the audiences before screening the movie. I took it to private homes, Messianic conferences and Israeli schools.

George Lauderdale, a friend from Georgia in the USA, had been corresponding with David Ben Gurion. The prime minister had an idea for a museum in Jerusalem, in which he wanted to show people the Old Testament basis of the Jewish, Christian and even Muslim religions.

I took George to the Negev where Ben Gurion lived at Kibbutz Sde Boker. Being at hand in case I had to translate, I was amazed at the ease with which this great leader conversed with us. *He's like a father,* I thought. *Here I am, chatting with one of the founders of the Jewish State!* When the conversation turned to the subject of Messianic believers, Ben Gurion said, "Yes, Jews believing in Jesus are still Jews!"

*A pity we didn't tape that conversation,* I thought when I realized the importance of his remark. After the meeting, pictures were taken. The man who filmed the interview insisted that I, too, should be in the photo shoot.

"An interview with Ben Gurion would also be great for the movie *Shalom-Salaam,*" Anita said when she heard where I'd been. "Irene, you interview him!"

"No!" I objected. "Let a man do the job of interviewing him."

This time we met with Ben Gurion in his library in Tel Aviv.

"Are you a Jew?" Ben Gurion bluntly asked the interviewer.

"No sir, but in my heart I am," the man answered truthfully.

"Well, that's the BEST!" Ben Gurion laughed. "You chose it, and not by accident of birth!" His face became serious. "When we don't need to study war anymore, we must teach peace in our schools. Let's hope that the Arabs feel the same way."

During Independence Day of 1972, I joined my neighbors in the yard outside the apartment to watch the military parade with tanks passing by. Bystanders cheered and waved flags, and together with those on the bleachers, we blessed the young soldiers and their commanders. I continued to pray for the peace of Jerusalem. My heart ached for the families of eleven Israeli Olympic team members who had been massacred in Munich by terrorists belonging to the Black Panthers. It was unbelievable, but the games continued as if nothing had happened.

It had been a difficult year for Israel. However, these hardships and heartaches were nothing compared to the trauma that was waiting around the corner of the next year – 1973.

Tent camp during the filming of our movie *Shalom-Salaam*.

The movie I showed throughout Israel.

Me, David Ben-Gurion and George Lauderdale.

# PART 8

# 1973 - 1978

The Israeli Defense Forces (IDF) were put in a state of high alert when the Egyptians advanced toward the Suez Canal in May of 1973. However, when it seemed the Egyptians were not preparing for war after all, the alert was cancelled.

The two-month summer holiday was over. Israeli schools had begun again on September 1st, and the Jewish population looked forward to the High Holy Days. First there was Rosh HaShana, the Jewish New Year, and a week later Yom Kippur, the Day of Atonement, followed by Succot, the Feast of Tabernacles. While the Jews prepared themselves for Yom Kippur, the holiest day of the year, Egypt and Syria prepared for war.

On the eve of Yom Kippur, Israel's leaders knew about the danger lurking at the Egyptian and Syrian borders. However, because Israel had been the first to attack Egypt in the Six Day War, they wanted to avoid international accusations of initiating another war against Arab states. The decision was made not to declare a full mobilization of reservists who now prepared themselves for a quiet day of fasting and prayers in synagogues.

# 36

## A 'Holy' War

"For the Battle is the Lord's." 1 Samuel 17: 46-47

On October 6th, Egyptian and Syrian armies simultaneously attacked Israel in the Sinai and the Golan Heights. On this day, nobody drove a car through Jewish Jerusalem, unless it was an emergency. Unaware of the looming danger, and not wanting to offend the Jewish people, in the afternoon I took a few of my guests to the Mount of Olives, in East Jerusalem, to give them a view of the city.

"What's all that smoke down there?" I knew something was terribly wrong. "We'd better go home. Perhaps the radio news will tell us what's happening."

Israeli radio and TV stopped broadcasting at the beginning of Yom Kippur, and now, at 2:00 p.m. the broadcaster confirmed what I had feared, "We've been attacked both in the north and south!"

I translated the Hebrew broadcast for my nervous friends. On the holiest day of the year, while the nation prayed in their synagogues and were weak from fasting, the enemies of the Jews attacked. The radio announcement was followed by civil defense measures.

"Total black-out," I translated. "Windows taped. No use of cars and telephones, except for emergency. Schools stay closed."

Men rushed home to exchange their prayer shawls for uniforms and hurried to assembly points. Soon, hundreds of vehicles drove through the previously empty streets to collect reserve soldiers. At the front lines, the regular army desperately waited for the reservists to join them. Some made it in fifteen hours, but for most it took at least twenty-four hours to reach their units. David Mills (a believer) and I drove to the police headquarters. "What can we do to

Around the world, believers fought on their knees for the Heavenly Host to stop the enemy. Syrian forces met little resistance and were only five miles (seven kilometer) from the Sea of Galilee when, inexplicably, they stopped. They could have easily continued into the Hula Valley. A similar situation occurred on the Golan Heights. After the war, it was revealed that military intelligence intercepted Syrian radio messages mentioning thousands of Israeli tanks, while in reality, there had been only a few.

A Sabra hitchhiker who accompanied me on many trips during the Yom Kippur War.

Destruction from the sky. A rocket had fallen just before we drove on a nearby road.

help?" we asked.

"Reservists must be taken to Tel Aviv," the man in charge told us. "All soldiers must be transported to their bases as well."

I had begun to fast and pray but knew that this wasn't enough. *O.K., I'll only fast partially,* I thought. If I were to be of use, I needed to keep up my strength and pray as I went. We drove straight to the collection point, filled the car with reserve soldiers and drove from Jerusalem to Tel Aviv and back again with more soldiers. While David drove, I sat in the back, talking Hebrew with the tense soldiers. Israel and the world held their breath. Would the enemies of the Jews succeed in wiping the little country off the map?

On October 7th, exhausted Israeli troops faced hundreds of Egyptian and Syrian tanks. By using their last ounces of strength, they were miraculously able to contain the invading armies. The Israeli High Command knew that the Golan Heights were to have high priority. The Sinai was a long way from the Israeli population, but should the Golan Heights fall, the Syrians surely would advance toward Tiberias, Safed, Haifa, Netanya and Tel Aviv. "These men urgently need to join their units at the Lebanese border," was another assignment.

I prayed for the men who were now facing death. "Lord, You are a shield around them. Arm them with strength. Enable them to stand on the **Heights!**" *What was gained in 1967 must not be lost now!* I thought.

That night, because the Syrians shelled Metulla, I joined civilians in a nearby bomb shelter. In between talking to frightened residents, I managed to get some sleep. The next morning I began the long journey back to Jerusalem. "The Lord is my rock, my fortress and my deliverer," I quoted from 2 Samuel 22.

Long lines began to form outside the supermarkets, as people were hoarding large quantities of bread and dairy products. A young Israeli hitchhiker learned that I was willing to drive to the northern frontline. He began to collect food from different shops, while I obtained toiletries, books and Bibles for the soldiers. When we reached the army camp, soldiers gathered around the car, and while the young Sabra handed out the supplies, I gave out the books, Bibles and whatever their eager arms would take.

The roads were badly damaged by artillery attacks, and the car was an easy target for the Syrians. We always prayed for the Lord to protect us, and He heard our prayers. We reached a section where, a few minutes before, a bomb had fallen on the road.

Each time I returned from a trip, anxious people bombarded me with questions about the situation at the front. Questions varied from, "How is the situation at the front lines?" and "Did you happen to see this or that unit?" to "Any news about casualties?" I could only tell them in general what I had seen or heard. The national mood was grave. This time Israelis felt that the country faced its supreme challenge. The word *meḥdal* – blunder - was in everyone's mouth. Families were fearful of the future. "Could you help get my children out to America?" a mother asked me.

On October 8th, my three seated Corvair, which I continued to drive since my days at the Carmel School, now shuttled soldiers from north to south. I drove all the way to Sharm el Sheikh, and back to Eilat and other fronts. God performed a miracle. Amikam, my spiritual son, was in one of the army camps, and I 'just happened to meet him there'. Together, we continued transporting soldiers and visiting camps.

An ever increasing volume of Egyptian tanks and troops kept pouring into the Sinai Peninsula. Special El Al flights brought hundreds of new immigrants to Israel, and many of them immediately joined the Israeli Defense Forces.

On the fifth day of the war, it seemed the scales were beginning to tilt in Israel's favor when the IDF found itself less than thirty-one miles ( fifty kilometers) from Damascus, Syria.

My car stood next to an Israeli tank that was pointing toward Damascus, alongside the Israeli command unit. I was reminded of Esther 9:1, "On this day the enemies of the Jews had hoped to overpower them, but now the tables were turned and the Jews got the upper hand over those who hated them."

The roads in the north were badly damaged, forcing me to drive slowly and carefully while dodging many potholes. Because of the frequent skirmishes, soldiers sometimes didn't allow civilians to continue on the roads. While waiting to be allowed to continue, I read Jeremiah 33. Finally, they allowed me to continue to the next army camp packed with soldiers. They were thrilled to see a civilian with a car full of goodies. At this time of year, it was bitterly cold on the Golan Heights and during the night, temperatures fell even below zero.

"Oh! Saḥlav!" The packages contained a popular Middle Eastern drink that was made from *salep* (orchid) flour. You had to pour hot water over the powder and each man would fill his cup with the thick drink. "Aaaaaah! This will keep us warm!" The battle-fatigued men sent me grateful smiles.

While the soldiers enjoyed their warm drinks, I encouraged them from the Scriptures I had just been reading. "'The days are coming,' declares the LORD, 'when I will fulfill the gracious promise I made to the house of Israel and the house of Judah'...." I continued reading from this powerful Scripture, emphasizing the "MAN upon the throne". They knew exactly to Whom I was refer-

David Mills (right), the Sabra hitchhiker (center) and I drove all the way down to Ophira (Sharm El Sheikh area) to take supplies to soldiers stationed there. Inside the heart on the t-shirt (center photo) is written: "To the IDF with love from Jerusalem". Soldiers were standing in line to write down addresses and messages for us to take to their loved ones at home. I kept those who were waiting occupied by singing with them.

Israeli soldiers, taking a break on their way to Damascus.

ring.

After giving them the gloves my Sheikh Jarrah fellowship had bought for these brave men, I told them I had to leave. "There are other army camps to bless and encourage!" I waved them good-bye and prayed for their safety. On my way to the next camp I passed Arab villages and Israeli settlements.

In addition to soldiers, we often had room for hitchhikers - one of my main reasons for traveling. One group of people hadn't been long out of the car when the next group entered. At another isolated army camp, soldiers swarmed around the vehicle. "What would you like us to bring next time?" I asked the soldiers who came to help unload supplies.

"The main thing is just your coming!" one of them replied.

Because Hadassah Hospital on Mount Scopus was still closed, many wounded soldiers were treated at the Ein Kerem branch of Hadassah Hospital. Donations from different Christian groups were used to help these men. Along with congregational leaders, we were invited to visit the hospital, in order to see what had been done with the contributions.

"What is this 'Sheikh Jarrah Fellowship'?" The tired looking doctor knew about the large denominations, and seemed interested to hear about our local fellowship.

"We are Bible believers," one of the believers we considered an 'elder' explained, "and we pray for the peace of Jerusalem."

"You don't know what this means to us!" The doctor was visibly touched. "Did you know that the Mount Scopus massacre happened in Sheikh Jarrah? Seventy-nine Hadassah doctors and nurses were viciously killed by an Arab mob, while the British did nothing to stop it or help the wounded."

"Isn't this amazing," the doctor said, "that from Sheikh Jarrah, you now bless Hadassah Hospital?"

From the way the doctor responded, I received Israel's 'stamp of approval'. Our fellowship of neighborhood Bible believers (no denomination, just gathered by region) helping the Jewish people, was God's way.

During these tense times, many people took refuge in my Tent of Abraham in Sheikh Jarrah. Two of them were new immigrants who had been too Messianic for their kibbutz's taste. There were also Jewish believers from Jack Hayford's congregation in the US. The cords of fellowship in the Lord were strengthened as neighborhood believers came together. Regardless of their backgrounds, Israeli or other, we began to take turns meeting at each other's homes. There were Arieh Paulson and the former pastor of St. Andrew's

Church, Gardner Scott and his wife. The couple had been persuaded not to retire but to become part of the local body of believers where they lived. We studied God's Word together, prayed and interceded, organized outreaches and gave neighbors a Christian welcome.

Kibbutz Moshabei Sadeh was situated not far from Sde Boker in the Negev Desert. The Griebenows had been missionaries in Tibet. Mrs. Griebenow, her daughter and I volunteered at the kibbutz for several weeks. There were many soldiers on the kibbutz and I noticed that most of the Hebrew songs they sang were about peace, and 'no longer learning war anymore', even though they were busy learning war maneuvers. Like everyone else in Israel, they longed for this war to come to an end. During the day, my friends and I worked in the kibbutz's ironing room. In the evenings, we were free to relax and have interesting talks. Mr. Griebenow had been invited by the kibbutzniks to show slides of their work in Tibet.

The crucial Mount Hermon outpost had become **the** symbol of the Yom Kippur War. "Did you hear?" people joyfully greeted each other. "The 'Eye of the Nation' is recaptured!" Mount Hermon was again in Israeli hands. Things were going well for Israel. UN Resolution 338 demanded a cessation of war and the start of negotiations to implement a 'just and permanent peace' in the Middle East.

On December 1st, David Ben Gurion, 'The Old Man' as everyone knew him, died of a stroke at the age of eighty-seven. More than 250,000 people came to pay their respects at the Knesset where his body lay in state. I was one of the many who had personally met him and experienced his greatness, with humility.

The Jewish New Year had begun with a devastating war that lasted over seven months. It was only on May 31st, 1974 that a disengagement agreement was signed between Syria and Israel. Finally, the Yom Kippur War had come to an end. The 2,569 bereaved families had to learn to live with their losses. For many Israelis, emotional and physical scars would haunt them for the rest of their lives.

# 37

## Blessing the World Through the Semitic Word

Richard Wurmbrand is coming to Jerusalem!" a friend told me. "He's visiting The Finnish School." I made sure to be there and it was at this meeting that I met Ada Reem, one of the daughters of Eliezer Ben Yehuda. When the two of us started talking we realized that we shared a love for the Hebrew language. It bonded us instantly.

It so happened that a Finnish lady who had been renting a room in Ada's apartment was leaving. "Would you like to rent the room? I live at 41 King George Street," Ada said.

I moved in with Ada but continued, together with capable lodgers, to oversee the Sheikh Jarrah apartment. It was still used to house a myriad of different guests. By traveling back and forth between East and West Jerusalem, I 'tied' the two parts together.

Yakir Am, a Jewish American, started Meditran, a club at the border of East and West Jerusalem, to bring Jewish and Arab youth together. It was similar to Father Bruno's group, which later became Neve Shalom. The participants learned about each other's feasts and languages. There and at other locations, they held joint second-hand clothing sales in Jerusalem. I often helped with these and other events.

Ada and I began to teach Hebrew to Arabs at the club. Pastor Milad, originally from Egypt and then pastor of an Arab assembly in the Old City of Jerusalem, asked me to teach Hebrew and the New Testament Book of Hebrews to an Arab youth group. Additionally, in Beit Jallah near Bethlehem, I taught a group of Arabs. It was so much fun when someone exclaimed, "Oh, I know that word! It's like our Arabic word!"

Ada and I often visited with leaders at Meditran, including a former Arab municipal leader and his Jewish wife. It was a hard blow for Yakir Am when the Meditran building was torched. He had done so much toward trying to reconcile Arabs and Jews and recorded the many events in a booklet.

"We're like Naomi and Ruth," Ada often joked. I was her driver, while she acted as my secretary when people who needed a place in my guest apartments phoned.

Since both of us wanted to learn Arabic better, we began reading Arabic large print New Testament booklets that someone had given me. There was an Arab from East Jerusalem's *Ecole Biblique* who wanted to learn Hebrew. So, during weekly meetings, a Jew, an Arab and an American were digging into the Semitic treasure house.

"Tents of Shem", we read and learned that the Hebrew 'tent'- *ohel*, in Arabic was *ahel* which meant 'family' in Hebrew. A tent and family go together.

Arabic *Naja* means 'redemption draws nigh', while the Hebrew *Noga* meant 'bright morning star' - Messiah who comes. "Unlike *Shalom/Salaam*/Peace, many words are not identical," I explained. "They are complimentary." I then showed them the beautiful connections. "We have the word 'rejoice'," I began. "Fara<u>H</u>, is the Arabic word. *Pera<u>H</u>* is the Hebrew word for flower or blossom." ("The desert shall rejoice and blossom".)

I let the words sink in. "Another example is the Arabic root for 'lamb' - *Hamal. Hamal Allah* means the Lamb of God. In Hebrew, *Hemla,* means 'compassion'. Now we have "the Lamb in His compassion.""

At the Sheikh Jarrah apartment, near the entrance I placed the following sign, with these plays-on-words: *Ohel-O* (His Tent – in Hebrew); *AHlan* (*Ahel* is family; *AHlan* is welcome in Arabic); Oh – hello! (is actual English). *AHlan* literally means: 'Feel a part of the family'. Jews love to use this expression.

> Ohel-O!
> AHlan!
> Oh – hello!
> Welcome to
> Abraham's Tent!

One of my teaching tools was a cloth chart that was held up by a stick. It contained maps of Jerusalem, Israel and the Middle East, and added to them was a page of these three-rooted Hebrew and Arabic words. The list on my folding chart became a huge blessing. People were amazed by the revelation of God's love and the grace that was embedded in the two languages. When I showed this in the USA, people were blessed, because it gave them a different view of the Middle East situation. The only thing they usually saw was Jews and Arabs fighting each other. Instead, the two languages blessed the world in the Semitic root of the living Word, free to all, whatever governments decided, or whatever war ensued because of land issues.

163

Ada often received visitors who were sent by the Ministry of Tourism. I served them tea while Ada told them about her father. When she was finished, she'd say to me, "Now you explain about the Hebrew prophets (and the Messiah)." which of course, I gladly did.

One of the places to which I often took my guests was the Ben Yehuda Museum and Hebrew Language Academy at Hebrew University. Because of my friendship with Ada, I got to know the extended Ben Yehuda family as well.

Dola was officially called Deborah, or Dvora, so named after her father's first wife and her aunt. As a child, unable to pronounce her name, she instead called herself "Dola", which means 'drawing out from a well', or 'from the work of her father', Eliezer Ben Yehuda. The linguistic isolation, because the Ben Yehuda children were only allowed to speak Hebrew at home, wasn't easy for Dola. "The dog and cat my father gave me were the first animals to understand modern Hebrew," she used to joke. Dola was allowed to marry a protestant, on condition they remained in the country and spoke only Hebrew. Max Wittman was an even greater devotee to Hebrew than Dola. He became an expert on the language and even when certain phrases were supplanted by newer terms, Max continued to use Ben Yehuda's original ones.

I often visited Dola and Max, who lived on Rehov Ahad HaAm. Their house was full of Ben Yehuda memorabilia – books, the famous sixteen-volume dictionary among them, and photos. I enjoyed the talks, meeting other guests, their favored cat, and having a 'cuppa' on their little porch.

I felt privileged being able to take the couple to their friends' or to other destinations in Israel. Once I drove them to Ginossar, a kibbutz on the shores of the Sea of Galilee, for a Jewish-Arab celebration with Yigal Alon.

Because of her fluency in Hebrew, Dola and I often discussed the treasures that could be found in one word, or root, or another. Often we looked up the Scriptures, and she would give me many hints from her teaching experiences to help me as I taught a Hebrew class. When I didn't know the answer to a question, I usually said, "I'll ask Dola."

Her father's sixteen-volume dictionary was our beacon, especially as she would point out the riches in the introduction. She loved to read to me letters that were sent by people praising the marvel of her father's work, and she never forgot to tell me that her mother, Hemda, also contributed to this 'master piece'.

"It's such a pity that the story about your father is out of print," I told Ada one day. "We should really get it back on the shelves, not only in English, but in Hebrew as well."

Dola and I paid to have Robert St. John's *Tongue of the Prophets* reprinted.

Visitors were
always welcome
at Ada's
apartment.

Ada Reem - a very
dear friend!

Ehud Ben Yehuda at his father's grave on the
Mount of Olives.

Dola and Ada,
on the street
named after
their father -
Eliezer
Ben Yehuda.

Even now I'm selling copies when I share about the historic struggle to have Hebrew accepted as the modern spoken language of the Jewish homeland. Jews returned to Israel from many lands and spoke the different languages of their nations of exile. It was the Hebrew language that united them.

Rivka Giladi asked me to write to the author to obtain permission for the creation of a Hebrew translation of *Tongue of the Prophets*. Once permission was obtained, Rivka did the translation and had the book printed in Hebrew. From her, I obtained the newly printed books which I then sold. I often took people to her talks at her retirement home in Ramat Eshkol, as she frequently covered Eliezer Ben Yehuda. While in her nineties, Rivka spoke without notes, in excellent Hebrew.

*Fulfillment of Prophecy* is the newer story of Eliezer Ben Yehuda, written by his grandson (with the same name), who added other particulars.

"Would you be willing to record excerpts from Ben Yehuda's story for a CD?" Brother Spiros from America asked. I happily obliged, and the CD has been given or sold in many places, especially in New York City.

Valentine (Val) Vester's family had been part of the American Colony established in Eastern Jerusalem in 1881. Val and Dola Ben Yehuda's family had been friends, but during the nineteen years that Jerusalem was divided, they had been unable to visit each other. When the city was reunited in 1967, I had the joy of often driving the two women to each other's homes, so that they could visit each other. They looked at photo albums and exchanged books about their parents' lives – *Our Jerusalem,* the story of Val Vester's family (the Spaffords) and *Tongue of the Prophets,* about the life of Ben Yehuda. Spafford was the author of the song 'It is Well With my Soul', the original penned copy now framed and displayed on a wall of The American Colony Hotel in Jerusalem.

My Sheikh Jarrah ministry had been the start of several other guest apartments that 'fell into my lap'. Across the street from where I lived, the Schiffmans rented an apartment from an Arab Christian landlord. The Schiffmans had been part of the local fellowship, but felt the Lord wanted them to return to the US. "Why don't you take over the rental contract?" they suggested. "And could you also buy our furniture and utensils?"

I felt this was from God, and agreed, paying them gradually through the guests' contributions. I created several bedrooms for prospective guests, who could also use the kitchen. There was a phone, to be used in good faith, and people paid what they could afford. Later, I suggested an amount that would help cover the expenses. Added to the blessings of that particular guest apartment was the fact that Bob Lindsey, head of the Baptist Church, and his family lived on the floor above. When people gathered up there for Bible study or prayer, he played his grand piano and would often introduce his newly composed songs, which echoed in the hallway below.

"Ada, would you be willing to tell my guests about your father?" I had been thinking about it for some time now. "It's a wonderful opportunity for the visitors to meet you." Ben Yehuda's daughter then told the story of her father's struggle to revive the Hebrew language, and after that I showed them the excellent film "His Land" which depicts the fulfillment of Biblical prophecy.

I loved the interaction with my guests. We shared news and prayed with each other. Many times neighbors joined us when a meeting took place in the guest apartment. I had the privilege of hosting several believers who later became famous in Israel and around the world.

"I'm new in Israel, and would like to learn Hebrew," Lance Lambert told me. I began to teach him and his friend the language of the Land at the guest apartment's kitchen table.

When Jim and Gwen Shaw first came to Israel, they found a home in the Sheikh Jarrah apartment. I enjoyed their friendship, and was thrilled when they began to bring groups to visit the Holy Land. Gwen established The End-time Handmaidens organization. I was often invited to speak to her frequent tour groups and helped sell her books.

"May I offer you a ride?" Soon the car was filled with grateful soldiers. "Where to?" I'd ask, and off I went, driving to their bases. It was natural telling them that I had just come from reading the New Testament with the daughter of the famous Ben Yehuda, and that I was now on my way to a Christian Arab meeting. I felt that what was implied in this was a very significant impartation as we'd elaborate on the subject.

Another batch of grateful young soldiers hopped in the car to ride back with me to Jerusalem. Mission accomplished, I looked at my watch. *Time to go to the Arab congregation.* I had offered to play the organ in the little church, and it had taken me some time before I got used to reading the music from right to left, to accompany the words that were printed in that 'other' direction. Before the meeting began, I went to greet the Arab pastor and put my bold request before him, "I'd like to ask for prayer for the Israeli soldiers."

Soldiers based in Jericho waited near the Old City's New Gate, to get back to the Jericho Police Station. During the many trips I made there and back, God often enabled me to share about the Author of Truth.

One day, while on our way to Jericho, an Arab driver hailed the car. I looked at the Israeli soldier sitting next to me. "Do you mind if we stop?"

"It's all right." He shrugged.

We loaned our jack and tools to the grateful Arab, who then drove to Jericho. At the army base another soldier waited for a 'hitch' to Jerusalem. I set out again, and everything went well, until suddenly the car stopped.

"Oh my!" I looked at the meter. "I've run out of gas."

Because we were in the middle of nowhere in the Judean Desert, the soldier caught a ride to the nearest petrol station and returned with a full jerry can. As he began to fill the tank, I heard a car stop behind us. My eyes widened when I recognized the driver. It was the Arab man we had helped earlier. Filled with wonder, I looked at the two men who were working together to fill the tank.

"You don't know how you two sons of Abraham have blessed this American!" I exclaimed when the job was done and briefly told them about the story of the Good Samaritan.

"Let's get you home now." I started the car and only then recognized the place where the car had stopped and where I had received help; It was at the Good Samaritan's Inn!

I could use my car to bless others in thousands of ways, and on my many trips throughout the land, the Lord always took care of me. I didn't have to lift a finger. When I had a puncture or mechanical trouble, somehow the soldiers or hitchhikers in the car always knew what to do. Years earlier, I often had a dream in which I walked, but so often didn't touch the ground. I wondered if it had been a kind of prophecy about my 'car ministry'. I didn't have to walk. It was the wheels that touched the road.

On one occasion I took two brothers from South Africa to speak at a church in Ramallah. While driving on the back roads I noticed the tank was almost empty and knew that there was no gas station in the vicinity. When I spotted an army camp coming up I was tempted to go in and ask for help but felt I should continue driving in faith. We reached Ramallah.

"I'll have to get some petrol here," I confessed. "The tank's empty."

My heart sank when I found out that the station was closed.

"Don't worry," said a man standing there. "We know one that's open. It's owned by a Christian."

Thankfully, it was downhill, so we coasted down on the empty tank, reached the petrol station, and filled up with gas. At the meeting, with great joy we shared about the miracle that God brought us safely there, and on time!

Valentine (Val) Vester (left)
and Dola Wittman (right).
Both holding each other's father's stories.

# 38

## Scattering Peace all over Jerusalem

In the course of God's surprising encounters, I had had the privilege of meeting and helping out special men of God, many of whom were Bible teachers. Two such men were Jacob Gartenhouse, who had a large ministry among the Jews, and Victor Buksbazen. Each had graciously offered his institution's support to me. Mr. Buksbazen was the Executive Director of the Friends of Israel (FOI) Gospel ministry. His wife Lydia's book and film *They Looked for a City* tell the story of how they helped Jewish refugees who were fleeing the Nazis. Dr. Buksbazen wrote many books, but a commentary on Isaiah was his masterpiece. I shared his love for the Word of God and his love for the Jewish people.

I often took the Buksbazens to visit the Kalisher family, whom they supported. We all became good friends. Zvi Kalisher wrote a book about his Holocaust experiences, and his life as a Jewish believer in Israel. During a meal at the Kalishers' I met an Iranian school principal. (Naomi Kalisher came from Persia.)

"Why don't you come and visit me in Teheran?" the Jewish friend asked me. In those days, there was still freedom for Americans and Jews to travel to there. Unable to go, I sent my friend, Gusti Weinberger instead. Later, I regretted that I had not taken the chance to visit Iran when it was still possible. Gusti was an Israeli who tried to bring Jews and Christians together, frequently hosting meetings in her home. She and I often took a Jewish mother and her children on outings and showed slides from Israel in many schools and absorption centers. We became good friends. I drove her many places, and one day we took *sufganiyot* (Chanukah donuts) to an army base. Another time we took Ada along to the Jericho army base, where she told soldiers about her father, Ben Yehuda. The young men listened as she shared about his work to revive the Hebrew language, one they had taken for granted.

One day a friend of mine suggested another 'guest-nest'. "There's a strategic center for rent in Abu Tor", he told me. "It overlooks Mount Zion and in the distance you can see the Walls of Jerusalem."

When I contacted the Muslim landlord, his answer was, "Very well, you can rent it, but only if you buy the furniture."

I thought about it. I had just been reading the Passover story in Mark 14. "Say to the owner of the house... 'The Teacher asks: Where is the guest room, where I may eat the Passover with my disciples?' He will show you a large upper room, furnished and ready. Make preparations for us there." (At this apartment for rent, there were steps to a large upper room.) A few weeks earlier, a believer from Haifa had given me a dinner set for twelve people because she was leaving Israel.

"Lord, this can't be a coincidence!" I saw it as God's green light to go ahead. I took a step in faith, rented the apartment and paid for the furniture in installments. A few weeks later, together with eleven friends (some Israelis), I celebrated an extra special Passover in my God-given 'Upper Room' in the Abu Tor apartment.

Gradually, special guests began to grace the apartment. There was Lurabelle, with her bags of teaching materials. I often accompanied her to homes and assemblies where, through use of small figurines, she told wonderful Bible stories. Bob and Lolly Grunska stayed there, too. Lolly had a puppet ministry, giving shows all over Israel.

"Let's plant some flowers," Lolly suggested one day. We worked hard to create a lovely garden, only to see that the next morning, everything had been uprooted. Showing them our willingness to forgive, we invited the neighbors to see the movie "His Land", and even served them refreshments!

"Do you know when the Baptists have their meetings?" a new guest inquired.

"Where can I find the St. George Cathedral?" another wanted to know.

"What time does the prayer meeting at Christ Church start?" a guest asked.

I decided it was time to make a list of congregations, their addresses and the times and languages in which they were held. The information chart was posted on the kitchen bulletin board.

"Could we have our wedding on the roof of your apartment?" Jewish friends asked me. "You've got an excellent view toward the Old City." It was also a perfect spot for social gatherings, a place where Mrs. Weinberger regularly hosted tea parties for her Jewish friends.

Another guest-nest was about to open up. Ada and I lived above a small ground floor apartment that was occupied by a young man.

"Wish we could do something about that noise," Ada complained, knowing full well there wasn't much she could do about it.

I asked the Lord to bless the young man and deal with the situation. Some time later, there was a knock on the door. "My downstairs apartment has become available," Mrs. Markson, the landlady, told me. "Would you like to rent it?"

"What happened to the young man?" I asked.

The lady made a dismissive motion with her hand. "Ah! He was always making such a noise! I told him to leave."

I began to use the additional place for my 'transients' – people who needed temporary housing and practical help. An American couple, Messianic believers whom I could help to learn Hebrew, had just immigrated. Today the husband, Yitzchak, delivers his sermons in Hebrew!

It didn't take long for my name as 'apartment hostess' to become well-known. Even the Ministry of Tourism heard about me! By word of mouth, news spread that I rented out apartments to people from all over the world.

"How do I know which apartment is the right one?" the new guest inquired when I handed him the key and explained how to get there.

"The one that has 'Irene' on the door," I said.

Then one day, I remembered that my name means "Peace" in Greek. *That's funny!* I thought and began to laugh. *I'm scattering peace all over Jerusalem.* One tourist couple made me a necklace with *"Shaloma"* in Hebrew, which I've worn ever since. (In Mark 16:1 we read that Salome -*Shaloma* in Hebrew - was at the empty tomb of Christ, Messiah.)

Ada heard and saw a lot of what was happening among the local believers. She liked the idea that people took turns having meetings in their homes, in our area of Jerusalem. When it was time for the ground floor apartment tenants to host the event, Ada joined the believers. Then one day, my open-minded friend said, "You can add my apartment to the list as well,"

I was pleased to hear my dear friend say those words. A few weeks later, Ada's apartment was ready to receive the believers.

"I suggest we kneel and commit this place to the Lord," brother Taine said before the meeting began. And to my surprise, neither Jewish Ada, nor I (knowing Jewish ways) objected. Brother Taine and his wife made *aliyah* and needed a place to live.

"Would you like to take over the rental contract of my guest apartment on

Schatz Street?" I asked the couple.

When the Taines moved there, the centrally located apartment, which had housed many tourists before, soon hosted many local gatherings. Especially during Pesach and other Jewish feasts, the couple's lovely apartment was always full of guests. And it was from this apartment that the Lord called Brother Taine to his heavenly home.

The last of my guest apartments was in the same building where I lived with Ada. This time it was the upper floor, not the basement. The owner had died, and the son, Mr. Yaffe, told me I could rent the furnished apartment on the fifth floor. He had one request – that I gradually take the hoard of books stowed in this apartment to his house. I didn't mind, and while I *schlepped* the books, a lovely friendship grew between the Yaffe family and me.

Even though it was a long walk up all those stairs to the fifth floor when the elevator didn't work, the apartment was soon used for all kinds of activities. A large room was created by opening the parlor's sliding doors to what I had made into an adjacent bedroom. Now I could show movies to neighbors and friends. I also invited Ada to tell the visitors about her father. This was the last guest apartment that I, later together with Lou, my second husband, operated.

Following the War of Independence, Israel's border with Lebanon had been quiet until 1970. Jordan expelled the Palestinian Liberation Organization (PLO), who then set up shop in southern Lebanon. During the Lebanese civil war, the PLO fought a tough battle with the South Lebanese Maronites for control over the area. Near the city of Metulla, in June 1976, a section of the Israel-Lebanon border was opened. Goods, workers and South Lebanese residents in need of aid began to cross at the Fatma crossing, which soon became widely known as 'The Good Fence'. Southern Lebanese residents, unable to travel to Beirut for medical treatment, were invited to come to Israel for help. Buildings appeared at the border post – a clinic, waiting rooms and reception areas, restaurants and even souvenir shops. The post was topped with national flags of both countries.

Israel provided the Lebanese with agricultural and veterinary aid, people received work permits for northern Israel, and schoolchildren visited sites in Israel. Soon thousands of tourists from all over the world flocked to the northernmost city of Israel to see The Good Fence for themselves.

# 39

## 'The Good Fence'

It often happened that I was asked to rent out apartments for friends who were abroad for a period of time. Visitors could take their pick from the guest apartments available, and after they had settled in, I would show them around Jerusalem. I often took them to different parts of Israel as well, and these contacts resulted in many friendships.

"I have to go up north," I told my guests. "Would you like to see the Sea of Galilee?"

The tourists were dropped in Tiberias. "I'll pick you up from here when I'm on my way back to Jerusalem," I promised, waving them good-bye. A couple of hours later I had reached Metulla.

Ibrahim, an Arab believer and liaison, often phoned to tell me of a need to transport Lebanese people to the hospital in Safed or Nahariya or back again.

When I reached The Good Fence at the Lebanese border, the people were already waiting for me. I had the privilege of witnessing spiritual healings taking place as Jewish doctors lovingly treated wounded or sick Arab Lebanese. Those who received treatment never forgot the compassion of Jewish doctors and medical personnel.

While at the Safed hospital, I could see the Sea of Galilee below – the place where Jesus had healed so many sick people. *You're still here Lord, healing hearts and bodies!* I thought.

A group of Israelis and international volunteers met regularly in Jerusalem to assess needs for financial help toward The Good Fence Project. Following is an excerpt from the minutes of a meeting of the Jerusalem Interfaith Committee for Aid to Lebanese War Victims, which was held on Tuesday, May 16th, 1978 at the Baptist House in Jerusalem. These minutes were respectfully submitted by Irene Duce Poe.

"Mr. Abu Leil gave a financial report and the outstanding needs.

1.) Families of seven people who were killed in Dible should be helped through a proposed sum of IL 14,000.(It was mentioned that the Baptist Village has received and cared for some, one lady for the term of eight months. Her son, who had been given up, was brought to complete recovery at Rambam Hospital in Haifa, now being discharged.)

2.) Several are in need of new artificial limbs... this would involve payment of about IL 35,000.

It was noted that ours is the only body working without screening recipients for religious tenets. There is help reaching South Lebanon from the Red Cross and others in Beirut. The Israeli authorities have helped with food, blankets, etc. Total finances needed for the current projects: about IL 147,000. As for the resources: Mrs. Schoneveld has some on hand. The sale of used clothing will be held May 19th at St. George's. Several letters with donations, totaling nearly IL 8,000 were just received. Mr. Abu Leil, seconded by Father Stiassny suggested that IL 35,000 be used for present needs. This is even advisable from the standpoint that the Israeli pound is constantly being devalued. The assistant driver of Ibrahim Siman, Mr. Hasham, was to receive IL 2,000 for an unlimited period. He also had many Lebanese staying at his home. Letters of appreciation should be sent to Mr. Wilbur Presson and Ray Register for their help in transporting patients also."

In view of all these expenses and urgent needs, I never asked for travel expenses. Most of the time God provided in miraculous ways. One day, the exact amount I had spent on gas for travel was returned as a gift - that same day. Mrs. Kofsman, who had not known about this expense, blessed me with a donation.

Often the patients traveled as a group, accompanied by a volunteer who helped them with crutches and wheelchairs. The Corvair was put to good use again, and when there was still room, I would also pick up hitchhiking Israeli soldiers along the way. When Israelis and Lebanese shared the same car, I found it natural to share about the roots of the Hebrew and Arabic languages. And of course, the conversation would be about the Bible and Israel as well. So many friendships with the Lebanese developed. One of them was with Frances Rizik, whom I visited at his home in Lebanon. Because he knew Hebrew, he often spoke at Israeli kibbutzim.

Because Haifa was much closer to the northern border than Jerusalem, I approached several believers. "Perhaps you, too, can become involved in these 'mercy trips'?" I challenged them. Some responded, like Wilbur Presson at Bethel.

I delivered my precious cargo from the hospital back to The Good Fence. "Till next time!" I waved to the leaders who were present at the border, Avraham and Ibrahim (their real names!), and began the journey back to Tiberias to pick up my guests.

"How was your trip, Irene?"

On the way back to Jerusalem, I shared the many blessings that I experienced in helping these special Lebanese and Israelis. And last, but not least, I told them about the wonderful things that were happening in the spiritual realm, and about how I had seen God's hand at work.

One day, while driving through the Jordan Valley toward Jerusalem, we heard a huge BANG! Thinking it had been the car backfiring, I didn't stop but kept on driving. Upon our safe arrival in Jerusalem, I saw that the car had been hit by a bullet – one inch from the tire. We realized that IF I had been forced to stop in the middle of Arab territory, we could have been killed by terrorists. God's guardian angels had been watching over us!

At the Good Fence, taking Lebanese patients
to Israeli hospitals.

On June 27, 1976, an Air France Airbus carrying 248 passengers was hijacked by Palestinian terrorists and forced to land in Entebbe, near Kampala, the capital of Uganda, Africa. They freed the non-Jewish passengers, held 103 people hostage and demanded that Israel release 53 convicted terrorists. By entering into negotiations with the terrorists, the Israeli government bought precious time needed to plan a seemingly impossible rescue operation. On the night of July 4, *Operation Thunderbolt*, also known as *Operation Jonathan* was launched. A C130 Hercules plane, carrying 100 elite commandos flew over 2,500 miles (4,000 km) to reach Uganda. During the ninety minutes it took to rescue the hostages, five Israeli commandos were wounded, and the hijackers and their Ugandan helpers were killed. The commander of the operation, Lieutenant Colonel Yonatan Netanyahu was killed. He was the older brother of Benjamin Netanyahu, a Knesset member and at times also Prime Minister of Israel. During the time of the raid, the American people were celebrating their independence gained in 1776. However, the centennial celebrations were overshadowed by news of the successful ending of the hijacking!

# PART 9

# 1978 - 2003

# 40

## Chosen to Bear Fruit

"You did not choose Me, but I chose you, and appointed you,
that you should go and bear fruit, and that your fruit should remain,
that whatever you ask of the Father in My name, He may give you."
John 15:16

> On September 9, 1978, a peace treaty was signed by President Menachem Begin, Anwar Sadat and Jimmy Carter at Camp David. It was also the year that Golda Meir died, and Refusenik Nathan Sharansky became a Prisoner of Zion when he was sentenced to thirteen years' imprisonment in the USSR.

I loved the song with which Israel, in 1979, won the Eurovision song contest for the second consecutive year. At this contest, many European countries presented their selections in their own languages. Israel's entry in 1979 was called "Hallelujah!" and Ada and I watched it on television.

The English translation is as follows, "Hallelujah to the world! Hallelujah all will sing, with one single word, the heart is filled with lots of thanks and it also beats out 'What a wonderful world!' Halleluiah with the song, for a day as it dawns, for what has been, and for what is yet to come – Hallelujah! Hallelujah for everything, for tomorrow and yesterday. All join hands and sing with a single heart – 'Hallelujah'!'"

Israeli drivers usually called each other *chamor!* (donkey) when they made mistakes. In the days that followed the song festival, they sang "Hallelujah" to each other.

During the Eurovision song festival, I had a 'dream': wouldn't it be wonderful if believers came together for a 'Jerusalem Vision', a communal 'sing-in', not for a prize, but for praise! Language didn't have to be a problem, for we could prepare translations ahead of time. In order to understand the words that were sung, people could pick up a written translation of each song in their own language folder as they entered the room or hall. There would be no speaker, only the beauty of those different languages coming together to worship the King. Babel would be turned into Blessing, in Jerusalem – the expression of God's best 'United Nations'.

On Thursday, February 5th 1981, after returning from the ecumenical English meeting, I had just wished Ada our usual *"Laila tov!"* (Good night!) when she came out of her room. "Could you phone Hediga [Hedva, her daughter] to get a doctor?"

I noticed she was having trouble breathing and heard her wheezing. "Can you hear that?" she asked me.

The Magen Adom ambulance took us to the emergency ward of Bikur Cholim Hospital, up the street, where her daughter and a friend soon arrived. About four hours later, at 3.30 a.m., Ada was gone. Ada's sudden passing came as a shock to all, as she had been active that day, though mainly at home. Many people remarked on the quick, quiet way she went.

"Death by a kiss", her neighbor said. "Only Ada could play a trick like that and take such a leap!"

Hediga phoned the family and put notices in the Hebrew and English newspapers, while I phoned many others and put a notice in the hall of our building. Because Ada had bequeathed her body to science, there was no funeral and no *shiva* (seven days of mourning).

A Jewish lady who was part of our Hebrew Bible reading circle, which Ada loved and co-hosted with me each week, suggested we meet. About twenty of us gathered to recall some of the many lovely things about Ada. It became a special 'memorial service', as people from all backgrounds recalled her words of wisdom, care for other people's problems, knowledge of many languages and many fields, and clarity in discussions. Ada was always optimistic, saw the best in people and was universal in heart. Even though she was proud to be Jewish, she hated the 'anti-Semitic' plea. She preferred to be called "Hebrew", as it went back further and related to the root of the Truth, God's Word.

Ada's humble home was a model of hospitality, as she warmly invited all types of people to stop by, and there was no need to notify her in advance.

While sipping their tea, every audience, whether one, two, ten or twenty people, was inspired as she told them of her father's work in renewing the Hebrew language. Added to that, she told the tourists of her own life ex-

Ada with Lea Ben Yehuda, widow of Itamar,
who was the first Hebrew speaking child in Israel!

The torched Bookshop
on Jaffa Street.

I loved to work at the bookshop and
meeting all kinds of interesting people.

periences in the land and abroad. This meeting was often the highlight of tourists' experiences in Israel. Ada wasn't a public speaker like her sister Dola, but she did give talks at an army camp and at an international school. She preferred to have conversations, answer questions and dive into the richness of the Hebrew words, in the quietness of her home.

During the seven years I lived with her, Ada showed and taught me so much. "Now let Your servant depart in peace," the Bible says, and Ada departed. In my spirit I could see myself hugging her on that great day, saying, "Oh, Ada! Here we are!"

There were so many good things that I had been able to share with my beloved Ada, and so many places we visited together. In honor of her special blessed memory, I wrote a leaflet about this special woman, with the heading from Psalm 87: "Of Zion, 'This one was born in her'." I altered it to read, "This one was born *and died* in her".

Ada and I used to walk over to her sister-in-law Lea's house. Lea had married Itamar Ben Yehuda, Dola and Ada's older brother, the first Hebrew speaking child. While visiting Dola, I often socialized with Lea's daughter Rina there as well. Rina was married to Avi Raz, who had a large pharmacy called Alba, on Jaffa Street. When the visits ended, I offered Rina lifts to her home, during which she always praised me for what I was doing for Dola.

Forced to move because of Max's ill health, Dola and Max moved to an apartment at the Sheraton Plaza Hotel. To these accommodations, I often took visitors from Israel and abroad, all of whom were touched by Dola's charm. They were happy to meet the daughter of the famous Ben Yehuda. One of Dola's favorite spots for me to take her was the King David Hotel.

I really missed my work at the Bible shops, and was glad to be able to volunteer at The Torch bookshop on Jaffa Street, not far from the central post office. This shop was very accessible to the public but sadly, later, it was partly torched by vandals. Thankfully, it was refurbished and went back into business.

It was 1980, and Israelis tried to get used to their new currency, the shekel, (taken from the Bible – 'weight'). Finally, they had their own currency. The Israeli pound, a reminder of the British Mandate, "Palestine", was history. Later, because of inflation, the shekel was changed to the NEW Israeli shekel, or NIS. Before the three zeros were dropped, we used to feel like millionaires.

```
                    "Shalom- Salaam"      (PEACE song)

Shalom,  Salaam Aleicum               Allah hu  Eloheem
    (Peace)                               (God)

Ben Adam hu Ibn Adam                  Avraham hu Ibraheem
   (Son of man)                          (Abraham)


Ahlan Wa Sahlan, Baruch Haba      Shukran, Fadl, Todah B'Vakasha
   (Welcome)                         (Thanks, please)

Walad, Yeled,  Um V Em ,  Abba V Abui Hem
   (child)      (Mother)    (Father)

  Yerushalayeem, Urushaleem Ilkuds
     (Jerusalem)

  Hamashiach, Il Massiach  V Daveed, Daood.
```

(explanation)
(Hebrew words
  underlined;       V- "and"            שלומה פה,)
 Arabic, not)      Hem- "they"          ת.ד.7438
                                         ירושלים)
        hu- "is"

When the Israeli government proclaimed Jerusalem the eternal capital, thirteen countries relocated their embassies from Jerusalem to Tel Aviv. Israel was deeply hurt by this slap in the face. During Succot that year, a number of Christians living in Israel were hosting a Christian celebration. During this time they felt God called them to open a Christian Embassy. Ever since then, the International Christian Embassy Jerusalem (ICEJ) has been a platform that represents Christians from around the world, speaking words of comfort and support to Israel, as well as providing practical means of help and support. ICEJ's presence states the fact that there are Christians who believe Israel's capital is Jerusalem, and not Tel Aviv; they support Israel's right to choose her own capital.

In the summer of that year, the Law of Jerusalem passed. The city of Jerusalem was to be the undivided, eternal capital of the State of Israel, established as such by King David almost 3,000 years earlier. Israel celebrated with tremendous fireworks over David's Citadel near Jaffa Gate. Together with friends, we watched them for over an hour. I had seen the announcements: "The heavens will shoot! – *Yeru shamayim"*. I likened it to *Yerushalayim* and smiled at the idea that "They will 'shoot' double peace" in Jerusalem, heavenly and earthly. Later, I always shared the following with my Hebrew students: From the root Y R H, one can create the word *Yoreh* (rain); by adding an M or a T to the root, you'll create a noun – *Moreh* (teacher). A teacher is someone who 'hits the mark'. *Torah* is God's Word 'that hits the mark'.

I shared Abraham's Tent and even my own room with Mrs. Coulson Shepherd. She and her husband produced TV programs about Israel in the USA. They had traveled with me through the Land, giving out God's Word. Around midnight we listened to Teddy Kollek's historical speech, "We made the song 'Jerusalem of Gold' and then we got all Jerusalem!" He had become the mayor of ALL Jerusalem – West and East – united again. "Maybe, if we make a song about peace, we'll get peace," Teddy Kollek said.

Those words inspired me that same night to write the song, "*Shalom-Salaam"*, with words of similar Semitic roots or meaning.

I taped this simple song, which was often sung during get-togethers, and gave it to Teddy Kollek.

The Mayor and his deputy, Benvenisti, explained to the public that the way Jerusalem could be kept united was by governing it by boroughs. It's not good to divide it between East and West. I totally agreed with Kollek's policy, and believed that this spiritual principle should be applied to the body of Christ as well.

One day I visited the mayor in his Rehaviah home, not far from mine, and when we talked on this subject, I compared the situation with the USA. That vast country isn't governed in a North-South division, (a reminder of the Civil War) but each state is separately governed under the capital of Washington, DC. I strongly believed the same principle could apply for believers of all denominations. "Wouldn't it be wonderful if we no longer used the labels Catholic, Protestant or other?" I said to one of the local leaders. "Instead, we'd have church gatherings of believers according to locality, under God's leadership."

Around this time, I happened to be in touch with three people who were named Paul. One brother had just arrived from the airport. Another was Paul Peterson, who wrote a book about the PLO. The third one was Paul Taine, a Jewish believer.

185

*What would the New Testament Paul do if he were here?* I wondered. The Scripture about Paul came to me - *He'd be "setting things in order".*

Weekly, a group of believers gathered at the Zion bookshop to study what the Bible has to say about the local church, from the New Testament. At the same time, I came across a book by Watchman Nee, in which he said that the best way to divide the body of Christ was geographically.

The more I thought about it, the more enthusiastic I became. I even wrote a short study about it. The church could best be divided by geographic locations, just like Israel would do well to govern by region rather than dividing as Israel/Palestine or East/West Jerusalem. Early church believers were not named after denominations but were named after the places they lived, like Ephesus or Smyrna. Through city-wide or nation-wide gatherings, in addition to weekly local gatherings, the Word could be preached, worship sung, testimonies given by the people, and prayers offered for the government, the army, outreach, etcetera. The gatherings would not be divided by race, but by **language** – clothed with the culture that goes with it. "Oh Jerusalem, put on your beautiful garments – out of the ashes," was the Scripture that came to me. The Body was important, but it was the garments of the Body that clothed it with beauty. The Word is important, but the cultural clothing of each language and nation or people group adds the beauty. We could visit other groups, since hopefully they would not be meeting at the same time. Spiritual communion could be enjoyed with other groups, even though they spoke a language we didn't know. This could be recorded for later translation. As Jews returned from many lands and languages to Jerusalem, each would have their own language 'nest', along with all learning Hebrew.

Floride Gant, a woman I had befriended in the 1950's, when she lived above us at St. Andrew's Guesthouse, was very much an 'evange**lust**', sharing the Gospel wherever she went, in restaurants, in the Old City, wherever! Floride had a rented a place on Ethiopia Street, several floors up. Visitors found it difficult to climb all those stairs. When a ground floor apartment became available, we helped Floride financially so she could rent the place. We called it The House of Prayer and you can see that name inscribed on a cornerstone of the building today.

Floride was on her way to the opening ceremony of the International Christian Embassy Jerusalem (ICEJ) at the Anglican School. When she came to the corner of Strauss and Prophets Streets, she was hit by a bus. The injured woman was taken to Bikur Cholim, almost across from there. The police were trying to find someone who knew her. She had a little notebook in her bag, and they found my name and telephone number in it. They phoned and told me

186

Floride Gant

Dola and me, probably at one of
her talks about her father.

Posing with my fiancée - Elijah (Lou) Levi

that a certain "Florida" was hurt and in the hospital.

"Who's that?" I asked.

"Well, she's seventy-two years old," the policeman added.

"Oh! Floride!" I exclaimed when it dawned on me whom they were talking about. I immediately went to the hospital and found Floride hooked up to a respirator. The only thing I could do was pray for my unconscious friend. Later, she was transferred to Hadassah Hospital where they could do more to help her. I took the Chandlers, who were in Israel during that time and also knew Floride, with me to visit her in Intensive Care.

A few days later, we were informed that she had passed away. The memorial service (I've never attended anything so beautiful!) was held in the Christian Missionary Alliance building, next door to Bikur Cholim. The service was attended by many believers who knew Floride, as she had lived in Israel for such a long time. Lance Lambert was the speaker. Those who knew Floride remembered certain things she used to do, and we all laughed. We just loved that dear woman! Between tears and laughter, it was a funeral that I'll never forget. She was buried in the Christian cemetery on Emek Refaim Street.

For the ICEJ, which Floride had supported wholeheartedly, it had been a challenge to obtain a much needed P.O. Box. In order to print letter-head, an address was urgently needed for Christians to support their new Embassy. However, in 1980, the waiting list for a telephone or a post office box was more than one year! Eventually, the ICEJ received a precious legacy from Floride, her no longer needed P.O. Box 1192.

A certain man had become a regular visitor to The Torch bookshop, where I continued to volunteer. Elijah 'Lou' Levi was a Messianic Jew from Alexandria, Egypt. He and his brother had recently made Aliyah. (I'm still in touch with his brother Moshe in Tel Aviv. His sister's family still lives in Egypt.) Knowing nine languages, Arabic and Hebrew among them, Lou joined me in witnessing to people visiting the shop.

Then one day, he said, "May I invite you out for a cup of coffee?" Lou took me to the coffee shop across the street. We began to share about our lives and when I mentioned that I had directed the Carmel School in Haifa, Lou was astonished. "You've been working with my son! He was a teacher there!" It was the beginning of a special relationship.

Ada had only recently passed away, Lou's wife gone. When Lou asked me to marry him, my fourteen years of widowhood came to an end. This, together with the fact that Egypt had made peace with Israel, caused me to feel in my heart that a new chapter was about to begin.

The only way a Jew could marry a non-Jew was either by way of the Consul of Paraguay or by traveling abroad. In 1982 we received our wedding license through a lawyer via the Paraguayan Consulate. Together with Jewish believers from a nearby congregation, we asked God's blessing on our marriage. Afterward we had a beautiful reception, prepared in Lurabelle's hospitable apartment. I had been 'at home' with this choice 'saint'. In her apartment, I'd participated in so many studies and celebrations.

Lou and I moved into the small ground floor guest apartment on King George Street, below Ada's apartment where I had lived after her daughter cleared it out, giving me many of her belongings.

It was a truly blessed year, for I also received Israeli citizenship. We had a good relationship with a woman at the Ministry of Interior and God used this contact to make this miracle happen. I'm still in contact with her today.

In was in 1983 that Lou and I moved to the Narkis Street apartment. Together with my husband I continued to look after several guest apartments. Lou also enjoyed the interaction with many guests, and participated in Bible studies and other activities.

"Don't you think we have 'washed enough of the disciples' sheets?" Lou asked me one day. It was time to let go of this ministry. The fifth floor King George Street apartment, which had hosted many, was the last to go.

Upon hearing that his neighbors, Ed and Gwen Carpenter were planning to join Pastor Joe Grana from Fullerton, California on a tour to Israel, Pastor Wurmbrand urged them to pay me a visit. "She will take you to meet my brother, Ebenezer," he promised them.

When the tour was over, Gwen, Ed, and their friends Joy and Dave Myers stayed for a few more days to do some additional touring. Hearing about their plans, I suggested, "I'll ask my good friend Hela, the tour guide, if she has time to take us to Shiloh."

In a seven-seater van, we drove to Shiloh, the area where the Tabernacle and the Ark of the Covenant once stood. Here, Hannah had prayed for a child.

"Our pastor's wife so longs for a child," Gwen said. "Perhaps we can pray for her here?"

Holding hands, we all believed and asked the Lord to give our sister in Christ a longed-for child. Gwen picked up some memorial stones from the excavation site to take home to California. And like Hannah had received her Samuel, the American pastor's wife was blessed by the Lord. She and her husband had a baby girl.

Our wedding in 1982.

Mr. and Mrs. Lou Levi
and friends.

At Dola's apartment, with
all the Ben-Yehuda
memorabilia.

Years later, Gwen wrote about her experiences in Israel:

*"Irene was like a bright shining star, going like a rocket around Jerusalem. We were amazed that she seemed to know everyone, and everyone seemed to know her. She invited us to her apartment, where we met her husband, Lou. This colorful man told us about Jerusalem. Irene is a rare jewel to our Lord Jesus, and we were amazed by this humble woman of God, who gives 100% of her life to work for Him in His Land."*

Another friend of the Wurmbrands, B.F. was also urged to look me up while in Jerusalem. He bought a double apartment complex in 'David's Village', near the Old City's Jaffa Gate. After both apartments had been dedicated to the glory of the Savior, many praise times were held there. I agreed to host a regular afternoon meeting, which usually lasted about two hours, and was visited by many local believers and tourists. B.F. was God's 'angel', who regularly helped me financially. Thanks to his generosity, I was able to continue offering my free Hebrew classes.

Dottie Lamont from Knoxville, Tennessee, was a friend of Gwen's. When she came to Israel in 1982, Gwen told her, "Dottie, you **must** meet Irene! She's been a helper in the Wurnbrand ministry."

So when Dottie phoned me from the hotel where she was staying, I went right away to pick her up and took her home with me. Dottie was impressed with meeting Lou, who sat talking to a Russian Orthodox priest. We had a wonderful time of fellowship, and I sold her a copy of *Tongue of the Prophets*.

In later years, whenever Dottie was in Israel, she would always try to visit me. "Being in the country without seeing you, Irene," Dottie said, "would feel as if something is lacking."

One day, I had parked our car in front of the YMCA building. Traffic was heavy on King David Street, and I knew there was no other way. I showed my passengers how Israelis handled such a situation. "Forgive me," I said, "but this is the only way I can get out, and you will see, the cars will stop. Lord, help me!"

Before the eyes of my astonished passengers, cars stopped and let me through. In Israel, we call this *chutzpah*, or nerve. Lottie thought I said *chuppah!* (a bridal canopy.)

Dola and I always stayed in contact with each other, and when I married Lou, we took Dola and Max all the way to Hamat Hader on the Golan. We also visited the Ben Yehuda home in Talpiot, where Hemda (Dola's mother) had lived for thirty years after the death of her husband. It was now used by German youth in a reconciliation project. I often took Dola and Max when they spoke at the Swedish Institute where they were honored participants.

Lou, Dola and Max while we were on a trip to the Jordan River and the Golan.

Dola in front of her family's home in Talpiot.

Israel's leaders knew that the only way to get some peace and quiet on the northern border was to attack PLO bases in Lebanon. In June of 1982, Operation Peace For Galilee was launched. The situation became extremely tense when Syria entered the war. With the help of Maronite leaders and the South Lebanese militia, the IDF was able to demolish PLO strongholds and expand the security zone. It was of utmost importance that Israel's north got out of range of PLO rockets.

For fifteen years, the Sinai had been part of Israel, and many people believed it shouldn't be returned to Egypt. However, with the signing of the Egyptian-Israeli peace treaty, Israel had no choice but to disengage from the vast area.

Northern Israel sighed with relief when in May of 1983 a peace treaty was signed between Lebanon and Israel. Israel got her security zone, a twenty-five mile (forty kilometer) buffer to the northern border. It was strange for the residents, not having to sleep in their bomb shelters any more. Now they could sleep in their own beds, in their own homes.

# 41

## God Cares for You!

"Cast all your anxieties on Him because He cares for you." 1 Peter 5:7

Weeks blended into months, then years. At the end of 1984 and through the beginning of 1985, Lou and I witnessed the joyful homecoming of more than 6,000 Ethiopian Jews through Operation Moses. In 1986, in the USSR, Nathan Sharansky was released from prison and that same day arrived in Israel.

Life in general had not become easier for my adopted country. In 1987, the *Intifada* (People's Rebellion) was the beginning of six years of rioting and fights between rock throwing Arabs and IDF soldiers. Knife attacks on civilians were small compared to attacks on busses that were plunged into abysses, killing and wounding many civilians. Jews became suspicious of Arabs. Upon leaving our houses in the morning, we were never sure to return alive in the evening. Lou and I trusted God to lead and protect us, and went about our daily tasks as usual.

In August of 1990, when Saddam Hussein invaded Kuwait, Israel began to distribute gasmasks to the population because the Iraqi leader threatened to use chemical weapons against Israel. "Never leave home without your gas mask!" the Home Front urged. Soon, people carried their defense kits with them wherever they went.

Everyone knew that another war was looming on the horizon. However, this time Israel was pressured by the USA to stay out of it. People were told to prepare a sealed room in their apartments, and instructed what to do in case of a chemical attack. Lou and I sealed our bedroom as well as we could. Lou didn't feel like wearing his gasmask. He decided to trust God that nothing would happen.

Lou loved to sit on benches around the city and strike up conversations with people about the Lord and Israel. Language wasn't a problem. He had enough to choose from. "How's your 'bench-ministry' going, Lou?" people often asked him.

Eating out at our favorite falafel place on Ben-Yehuda Street.

Outside our home on Narkiss Street.

The IDF's hands were tied, and the country was a sitting duck when on January 17, 1991, eight Scud missiles fell on Tel Aviv. Sirens went off and everyone rushed to their sealed rooms. Nobody knew if the Scuds carried chemical warheads. Together with the anxious population, we were forced to wait a few hours in our sealed room until the 'all clear' sign was given. Radios and TVs were always on, and the moment sirens went off again, people rushed to their sealed rooms. Nahman Shai, the son of my dear neighbors, became a beacon on Israeli TV. In a calm and controlled way, Nahman told the anxious population when to put the gasmasks on, and when to take them off again.

After a few days, it became clear that most Scuds were aimed at the greater Tel Aviv area. They caused much property damage, but miraculously, no people were killed during these attacks. Before the Gulf War, most people preferred to be in 'safe' Tel Aviv. Now, many rushed to the safety of Jerusalem. It was a tense time, but Israelis were determined not to let their lives be ruled by terror, even when it came from the sky. People went to work, children to school, and life continued as usual. And if the siren went off while you were in a checkout line at the supermarket, you just left your groceries where they were and left for shelter, to return when the all-clear sounded.

To me, it seemed ridiculous to be wearing the mask, especially when we were at a prayer meeting when the sirens went off, and our prayers were muffled by the gasmask.

That year, the Purim celebrations were extra joyful. The Jewish people didn't see it as a coincidence that the Gulf War ended on Purim. The new Haman (Saddam Hussein) had been defeated.

Lou and I rejoiced with the country in May of 1991 when Operation Solomon brought 14,000 Ethiopian Jews to Israel. Within thirty-five hours, El Al and military planes performed more than forty airlifts to bring the people home. The miracle brought tears to many eyes. After years of separation, families were reunited. The new immigrants, called *olim*, were dispersed among absorption centers around the country. Together with a Jewish neighbor, I visited the absorption center in *Givat HaMatos*, on the road to Bethlehem. We took clothes and food and ministered the Word of God to these *olim*.

In 1993, I was invited to speak to a group at a hotel in Jerusalem. There, I met Kay Mercuro from Washington, DC. "I'm planning to go on a trip to India," Kay said. "Would you like to join me?"

My heart jumped with joy! The 'goal' I'd had of being in India was coming true. Many years prior, I had thought the Lord wanted me to minister to the Jews in India, but I had been led to Israel instead. I shall never forget these

The Madrid Peace Conference was held from October 30 to November 1, 1991. The United States and the USSR co-hosted a conference in Spain, to set the framework for peace negotiations between Israel and Jordan, Syria, Lebanon and the Palestinians. Since 1949, these were the first direct and open peace talks that had been held between Israel and these four partners. By now, Israel's enemies had learned that suicide bombers blowing up busses created more terror and havoc than just plunging a bus into a ravine. Hamas and Islamic Jihad, disagreeing with the Oslo Accords, signed between PLO leader Yasser Arafat and Yitzhak Rabin, carried out one horrific terrorist attack after another. Despite the ever present danger, there were always a few brave tourists who continued to visit Israel. They wanted to show their love toward and solidarity with the Jews, and in turn, were blessed by the Israeli public.

On September 13, 1993, The Oslo Accords were signed. Israeli Prime Minister Yitzhak Rabin and Palestinian leader Yasser Arafat shook hands over the "land for peace" strategy outlined in the Oslo Accords. Arafat pledged that the PLO recognized Israel and committed itself to peace, while Rabin stated that Israel recognized the PLO as a legitimate party in negotiations for peace.

From left to right: Eleanor Cates-Rousseau, Eunice Helin and Dola enjoying a lunch at my home.

humble Indian people – their rickshaws, the rice dishes, but especially their kindness, and the gifts of saris to wear.

Along with many Israelis visiting India, we flew to Bombay where we spent a few days. From there we traveled to Trichy, south of Madras, where Kay knew a pastor. Those beautiful Indian people, most of them sitting on the floor, listened attentively as I spoke about Israel. We were able to help out in churches and during conferences, not only there, but also in Madras. Back in Bombay, we again encountered Jews, visited their synagogues, shared a meal with them, and spoke Hebrew with some. On our way home, we went by way of Egypt and visited Lou's sister Janet who, when she visited Israel, was called Esther. Together we rode down the Nile and enjoyed getting to know Janet, her family and friends better.

My friend Kay returned to the States, but I stayed another day. While riding the subway, someone asked, "Do you believe in the Son of God?"

Under the impression that the man was a believer, I happily answered, "Yes!" Suddenly the atmosphere in the full compartment became hostile and everyone seemed to turn against me. "God has His way of revealing His truth to those who want to know!" I added, sighing with relief when my answer helped diffuse the tense situation - as I could see those Muslims seemed ready to attack me.

Now that Jordan and Israel had signed a peace treaty, there was nothing that could stop me from going there. It brought back so many precious memories. I was thrilled when my friend Kay took me to see Petra and Aqaba near the Red Sea in Jordan, and other places. During the time Stanley and I had lived in Amman, we had not visited those special places, as we were too busy helping refugees. It had been so many years since I had been in Amman. Seeing how much it had grown, I had a hard time trying to find people we had known. While there, Kay and I attended a lively fellowship of Arab believers.

The only thing Israel wanted was to live in peace. Prime Minister Rabin had been willing to make huge territorial concessions in order to obtain a worthless 'promise' for peace and security. The world was stunned when, in November of 1995, he was assassinated. From all over the world, people flew to Israel to attend the funeral.

"*Shalom chaver!* – Shalom, friend!" American President Bill Clinton ended his eulogy. Soon, Israeli cars could be seen with bumper stickers carrying those words – *Shalom, chaver!* The collapsed 'Peace Process' inaugurated another wave of suicide bombers, killing and maiming innocent civilians.

Seventy-seven year old Lou's health was deteriorating to such an extent that he had to use oxygen tanks. These were brought to our house by a young Israeli, and we also had regular visits from our *Kupat Holim*, or health fund doctor. Because of his medical needs, Lou was no longer able to go out and meet people. Instead, they came to our house. The many deep spiritual conversations we had with visitors and friends brought us closer together. By car I often took Lou in his wheelchair to the hospital where he received blood transfusions. Often we were there at the same time as Sam Frieden, another Jewish believer.

The Lord called Lou home in April of 1996. The hallway of our apartment building that had hosted so many of our visitors was now filled with people who came to sit *shiva* with me.

I had been married to Stanley for twenty years, a widow for fourteen years and then the Lord had given me Lou. We had been together for fourteen years, and now, at the age of seventy-six, I had become a widow again. I took a conscious step in faith to leave the details of my future in God's hands.

1993 - Kay Mercurro and our Indian friends.
On the right, Pastor Genarish.

# 42

## Beckoning the Gentiles

In the days and weeks after Lou's death, believers and friends surrounded me with their consolation. Then one day, Lillian Williams invited me to go to the USA. She had a radio ministry and when visiting Israel, always came to see me. We ministered especially to a policeman's family whom she had helped in Tiberias. Of course, we showed the film "His Land" there.

On my US trip, I was invited to speak in several American churches and knew that the offerings I received should be set apart for the church in Jerusalem. *The personal gifts I'll use for my own needs,* I thought. When it was time to return home, my plane took off around midnight, so I began to read my daily Scripture portion for the new day – 2 Kings 12:14-15. The verse spoke about giving to the workmen for the repair of the house of the Lord. Reckoning wasn't necessary, they dealt faithfully. *What a timely verse,* I thought and looked up my New Testament reading for that day - 1 Corinthians 16:1-3. "Concerning the collection for the saints... I will bring your liberality to Jerusalem!" I was awed by what I read. The donations from the churches where I had spoken and which I felt should be designated for the church in Jerusalem, were of the **same amount** as the money friends and relatives had given me for my personal needs.

I knew that God wanted me to use the donations for Jerusalem in a three-fold way. It was clear that 1/3 of the sum was to be given to a representative of the Hebrew assemblies, 1/3 to the Arabic believers, and 1/3 to a gathering of leaders of English-speaking congregations. With the donations, I added the verse from 2 Kings 12:14-15 – no need to give account! I trusted them to deal faithfully.

On Thursday evenings I always went to a charismatic meeting that had developed, binding believers together in spiritual renewal. Regardless of our church backgrounds, we worshipped God together. I shared about my experiences in America, the freedom we had, and shared a song that came to me of "Our One Savior and Supplier!"

Two Jewish believers, both named Paul, with whom I had shared God's vision for His best, had each given me large, unsolicited donations. At the Thursday evening gatherings, I felt led to give one check to a leading brother who would use it in his area of Jerusalem. The second check went to another brother who had a ministry in another area. I trusted them to use it for ministering to God's people in their local gatherings, feeling more and more that His Body is divided by location, not denomination.

For years, believers from all over the world had been praying for an end to Communism. Here in Israel, we especially prayed for the Jews to be able to return to their land. When the Iron Curtain finally came down, the 'Second Exodus' began. This time, Jewish people streamed from the Soviet Union and all of Eastern Europe.

In the Soviet Union, assimilated Russian Jews were still identified as Jewish by nationality. If both parents were Jewish, they were too, a fact that was clearly demarked on their ID cards. The Communist regime made them easy targets for anti-Jewish discrimination and later they suffered terribly under Stalin's undisguised anti-Semitic policies. Soviet Jewish youth became aware of their Jewish roots and emotional attachment to the newly established state of Israel. For them, it was the only place where Jews could live a normal life and be proud of their heritage. Many applied for visas, but didn't receive permission to leave the Soviet Union. These people were called *Refuseniks*.

Englishman Phil Hunter had a Christian bus company called Good News Travels. After he had been in Israel and behind the Iron Curtain, God spoke to him through Isaiah 49:22. "This is what the sovereign LORD says: 'See, I will beckon the gentiles, I will lift up My banner to the peoples. They will bring your sons in their arms and carry your daughters on their shoulders'."

About the same time, another group of Christians had created the Ebenezer Fund, in order to bring Jews home by ship.

Phil knew that God wanted him to use his coaches to bring the Jewish people out of the Former Soviet Union and Eastern Europe and, in coopera-

1998 - Kiev - Exobus. Witnessing the tearful good-byes to friends and families, who are on their to Israel.

1998 - Anita and her relatives' home overlooking Beirut.

tion with the Jewish Agency, bring them to Israel. The first trip of Exobus, his new ministry, was made in 1990. In the months and years that followed, Exobus' multi-national staff learned to deal with difficult road conditions, authorities, mafia, immigration control and customs.

Anita, my friend who made the movie *Shalom-Salaam*, and I joined a group working for Exobus by accompanying them on a trip to bring Russian Jews to Israel. We went to support and pray for the Jewish people and their immigration. Via Turkish Airlines I flew from Israel to what had been 'enemy' Russia. Because Anita knew a pastor in St. Petersburg, then called Leningrad, we went there first. There, we visited two important church groups. One was Messianic in character with Hebrew songs and much teaching. We also spoke to another group and used Israeli teaching materials. It was wonderful to be in touch with many individual believers. I remember well the deep elevator rides in the metro station and getting a taste of Russian life. It was especially significant, being beyond the American-Russian Cold War.

Joining the Exobus team in Germany, we then traveled to Poland, where I learned about the awful past of the Warsaw Ghetto and the persecution of Jews there during the Second World War. On our way to the Russian border, we also visited Majdanek, a former Nazi concentration camp on the outskirts of Lublin. Seeing the piles of ashes and ovens where their bodies were incinerated deeply touched me, even more when I learned about the gruesome history of the former labor camp. Even though it had operated for only thirty-four months, 80,000 people had lost their lives there, and 59,000 of them were Polish Jews.

Soviet Jews wanting to make Aliyah had to travel to cities where the Jewish Agency had established centers. They were in Leningrad and Moscow. Those from Siberia had to travel to Kiev. Transported by Exobus from all over the area to the Jewish Agency Center, people were processed and then flown to Israel. These centers were also used to teach prospective immigrants about Israel, the culture, and life there. Watching films about Israel gave them hope, like when they saw youth dancing the *Hora,* a well known Israeli folk dance.

Anita and I witnessed tearful good-byes and noticed that friends and family who stayed behind kept waving till the bus was out of sight. Inside the bus, the atmosphere was heavy, as the Jewish travelers realized the enormity of their decision.

Besides practical assistance, the Jewish passengers also needed moral and spiritual support. They left behind lives, family members, and their families' graves. Their homeland had been like a mother to them. What they faced now was an unknown future in a new country. Sorrow and joy were conflicting emotions.

"All over the world there are Christians who love the Jewish people and are praying for you," the Exobus staff told the passengers, and they distributed Scriptures that explained God's ingathering to them. Upon hearing that I lived in Israel, people bombarded me with questions. I also had the privilege of sharing God's love and promises with them and even taught them a little Hebrew. After having seen the death camp, it was such a blessing to be able to serve these new immigrants. The Jewish people were coming back to life!

Later, when I met some of my friends from this trip again in Israel, we shared addresses and meals.

After being with the group and Exobus in Kiev, Anita and I traveled overland via Europe to England, where I visited Stanley's family. My traveling days were not over yet, but were of a different nature. Because of the political situation, the only way I could join Anita to go to Lebanon was by traveling via Cyprus. It seemed like a lifetime ago that I had been on the island.

In Lebanon, Anita had a relative who worked among handicapped youth in Beirut. Through creative, productive work he encouraged the young people to live an independent life, as they sold their crafts. One of the Arabic leaders took us to Sidon where, in 1948, I had worked among Arab refugees in the camps. It was such a joy to visit Bhandoum, where I had lived. The man I remembered as a little boy now had a thriving pharmacy. We went further south to visit points where Israeli forces had been. We kept seeing demolished homes and villages – sad reminders of the Lebanese civil war. So much had changed.

In their churches as well as at a villa overlooking the port of Beirut, we had fellowship with Maronite believers. These precious people prayed hard for peace with Israel. Anita and I drove to northern Lebanon, where Maronite believers had another meeting place. While there, of course we also took time to see the Cedars of Lebanon. The lurking fear of Syrian infiltration, even during the elections, kept the believers looking to the Lord above.

1999 - Celebrating my eightieth birthday with friends.
From left to right: Heinz Pollack, Victor Shmadja, wife of Sam Freyden,
Meg McCollumn, me, Miriam Genevoir, Susie Shmadja, Gavriella Pollack.

Getting ready for the next group of students.

# 43

## God's Presence, our Strength

*'It is not just the sense of God's presence,*
*but the fact of His Presence that is our Strength'*

From the moment Israel had occupied southern Lebanon following the 1978 Lebanon War, the world put pressure on her to pull out from the security zone. Likewise, Hizbollah, a Syrian sponsored terrorist organization, worked hard to oust Israel from the zone that protected northern Israel. 'Helped' by the UN, it had come to pass after twenty-two years that Israel agreed to leave in May of 2000. Not only Israelis dreaded the pull out. Hundreds of Christians, Druze and Muslims had been fighting alongside the IDF, protecting their villages. Fearing for their lives, over 7,000 Lebanese fled, finding a safe haven in Israel. The Good Fence was closed. What was left was a memorial of a unique era gone by.

Beverly Timgrin, a friend of Anita's and mine, had set up a dental clinic in Marjayoun, Lebanon, north of the Israeli city of Metulla. Beverly joined the exodus of Lebanese people whom she had served for so many years. I took her into camps, hotels and homes all over Israel that had been designated for the thousands of Lebanese refugees. Wherever we went, Beverly, who is fluent in Arabic, encouraged the distraught people and saw to their physical needs as we distributed many necessities and treats to the children. Clothes were distributed, government help came forth, and gradually, the Lebanese refugees began to adjust to their new situation and to learning Hebrew. Beverly was able to set up a new dental clinic for the Lebanese in Tiberias and families whom we met could be helped with clothes and equipment.

I never received compensation for the cost of driving Beverly around in the car Anita provided. However, the hundreds of experiences I had while accompanying her on visits with the Lebanese people and authorities who assisted here were, to me, more than enough payment, and God supplied for all.

"Would you be willing to take these reporters into southern Lebanon?" a government official asked me one day. "I'll make sure you will have all the necessary permits." I made several trips, and even took journalists and others to the 'Voice of Hope' This was a radio station ministry founded in 1979 by George Otis, who began broadcasting in South Lebanon in an embattled area. What started as a small radio station evolved into a global broadcasting network with bases throughout the world. We also drove to the Mia Mia camp near Sidon, where I had worked in 1948.

When it was clear that the Lebanese refugees couldn't return to their villages in southern Lebanon, Israel offered them citizenship. It was such a joy for me to participate in a Chanukah/Christmas party on a northern kibbutz for the Lebanese people. The party was organized by the widow of Major Haddad, who had been head of the Southern Lebanese army.

The death of King Hussein of Jordan and Hafez Assad in Syria created another set of internal changes that Israel's leaders watched with a hawk's eye. The renewed peace talks at Camp David between the PLO and Israel collapsed again, resulting in the Second Intifada. But terror wasn't only confined to Israel. The 2001 attack on the World Trade Center in the USA opened the eyes of many to the severity of this global threat.

Dola continued to live in the Sheraton Plaza Hotel after Max passed away. Daisy Aziel was sent by the health fund to become Dola's caregiver. The three of us often had a meal together in the hotel's dining room, where workers would greet her as a friend. Dola loved it when I took her to Mevasseret to visit

Daisy and her welcoming family. She always enjoyed the views of the lovely countryside and marveled at Jerusalem's growth.

After Dola had a fall, her family told her she would need constant care, and arranged for a Filipino girl to come and stay with her. When the helper had to go somewhere, I often sat with Dola at her table, reviewing the family pictures laid out in front of her. Together we would reminisce, since I knew most of them. "You are the closest to me now," Dola once said. We often discussed the news, as she kept up with her daily newspaper. At times we also touched on God and heaven. What other gift besides a weekly bouquet of flowers could I bring my friend at her centennial age? How could I show her my extreme gratitude for the revival of the Hebrew language? She always blessed me with her welcoming smile.

In 2003, Dola passed away at the age of 103. I felt bereft after losing another dear friend. Like her sister Ada, she, too, donated her body to science. Later, her remains were interred in the Emek Refaim Alliance Cemetery together with her husband's, in accordance with her will. She is one of the few Jews buried there. At the time of the burial I saw many of her family members and friends. The couple's gravesite lacks a tombstone. Rather, it has just a tiny sign with their names on it.

Dola and Max Wittman had no children, and became benefactors of the Hebrew University of Jerusalem. I went to the memorial service which was held at the university's Mount Scopus campus. Daisy, her faithful caregiver, was there, along with many others who had known and loved Dola.

On my birthday in August of 2003, I reflected on my age – 84! I was grateful that God had already granted me such a long time on earth. It had been seven years since I had last visited the States. God arranged my next furlough through Anita's inviting me to share at her Messianic art week. I visited many friends and contacts in Virginia, Florida and California and, of course, caught up with my sisters. All of them were still in good health.

We five Poe girls had long ago begun writing our so-called 'Round Robin letter' in order keep in touch with each other, since four of us had scattered. Only Alyce remained in Ohio. Carol would send the first letter to Mother and Alyce, who added theirs and sent them on. The Round Robin cycle had begun! The envelope would contain a letter from each sister who had exchanged her previously written letter with an updated one, and sent it off to the next sister. Following is an excerpt from Carol's book, *My Chunk of a Century:*

Dola at the age of about one hundred! She always greeted me with a smile.

Teaching Hebrew gives me so much joy!

Round Robin letters with some last pictures of Aunt Naomi, before she passed away.

**February 6, 1945**
Dear Girls,
No, Mom I am NOT going to write "Dear Girls and the Old Lady."...
I'm taking it to mean us all. OK? Forgive me for raving about this beautiful spot... It smells like April outside. We plan to put in a garden soon.... They had left Ohio and were now living in Southern California.]

**March 21, 1945**
Dear Mom, Irene, Mary, Edna, Alyce,
What a lineup! As I write the names down one by one, I get the feeling a miser must have when he counts his gold pieces. I miss you. Your letters buzz with talk of get-togethers at which I will be absent. Mary and Irene are coming to McComb for a weekend. Edna is coming home this spring....

**April 12, 1945**
Dear Robins,
Guess what! It's raining! But yesterday and Monday were so beautiful it took my breath away.

**May 16, 1945**
Dear DEAR Girls,
Gee, you letters really turned the trick this time, and after I'd boasted that I hadn't been crying with homesickness yet. Does anyone know who said "To go away is to die a little"? But I WILL see you all again or know the reason why. Now don't all start telling me the reasons why! I want to enter a protest. You kids are always saying things that pique my curiosity rather than satisfy it.

**September 7, 1945**
Dears,
Hi! Look, Mary, a new typewriter ribbon! Now quit scolding. I'm having to get used to not hitting the keys with a hammer. Irene, do you have an MA after your name now? Next it will be a PHD and we'll have to call you Dr. Poe. Just think, in only a week or so, the Poe family will have three titles, RN (Registered Nurse) MA (Master of Arts) and MRS.

When our mother passed away, we sisters decided to continue with our Round Robin letters, and asked Aunt Naomi to join us. These Round Robin letters have circled the globe for more than sixty years now!

While I was in New York City, Anita invited me to join her for the Helsinki Jewish Evangelism Conference and afterward for an organized bus tour through Finland. It was my first visit to Scandinavia. I was thrilled to see the North Cape and even Lapland, and fell in love with the beauty of Finland. I looked forward to telling the Finnish workers in Israel where I'd been. It had been a wonderful trip, but I was grateful when the El Al plane took me home - to Israel!

2003 - Finland
With Anita at the Helsinki Jewish
Evangelism Conference.

Catching up with the Wurmbrands while I was visiting America.

Taking friends to see the Ben Yehuda museum.

# PART 10

# 2003 - Present

# 44

## The Golden Years

After I stopped being hostess for the guest apartments, it had become an integral part of my life to oversee apartments and collect mail for absentee landlords and owners. At the time I had stopped my guest apartments, the Wurmbrands referred me to Bill French, a faithful servant of God. "Would you like to oversee this lovely Bible-centered apartment while I'm abroad?" he asked. He suggested I use it then for afternoon worship meetings with instruments, testimonies, etcetera, all to the glory of God. This brother in the Lord is proof that my Father in Heaven supplies!

I was willing to do everything for the cause of peace. After the 1967 War, I had often been in Gaza City, where I fellowshipped at a Baptist church. Many parts of the Gaza Strip had been vitalized by Jewish groups with beautifully built settlements. In doing so, this provided employment for many Arab workers.

In my capacity as a teacher, I worked bringing Jewish and Arab schools together on their common denominator - the Old Testament. There was a school in Ramot, the northern part of Jerusalem, where I volunteered to teach English for special groups. The school had been named after Yonathan Netanyahu, the commander who had been killed in 1976 during the Entebbe raid. In this school, we teachers were planning a get-together with an Arabic school. We had good relations, until the day in February of 2005, when security authorities foiled a double suicide bombing that had been planned. Bags containing explosive charges placed in cardboard boxes were found, and in order to increase the damage to victims, the material had been supplemented by nails and shrapnel. The plan had been for suicide bombers to infiltrate Jerusalem's Ramot neighborhood in order to carry out attacks in buses, a synagogue, or coffee shops.

Upon hearing about these thwarted attacks, our desire to go on with the project subsided. However, I continued to teach in this Jewish school. Every time I drove to that school in Ramot, I always carried a little poster saying, "He hangeth the earth upon NOTHING", taken from Job 26 verse 7.

In 2005, after having been in the Gaza Strip for thirty-eight years, the IDF pulled out, endless entreaties and demonstrations notwithstanding. However, instead of longed for peace, Israel was treated to a continual barrage of rocket attacks from the Gaza Strip onto Sderot and surrounding areas. The Hamas (meaning violence) was behind it all.

It seemed that every time a leader agreed to give away part of Israel, something happened to him. Rabin had been murdered, and in 2006, Ariel Sharon suffered a brain hemorrhage, which left him in a vegetative state.

Ever since Israel had pulled out of southern Lebanon, the north increasingly suffered under Hizbollah rocket attacks. Israel was forced to retaliate and in July of 2006 launched the Second Lebanon War. During this time, many Israelis from the north had taken refuge in reduced rate Jerusalem hotels, where I visited many people whom I knew, often taking them to see the sites. The thirty-four day military conflict ended in September, and restored some peace and quiet to northern Israel.

# 45

## Singing 'Hallelujah!'

In 1969, after Stanley's home-going, I had returned to Israel. In August that year, TWA flight 840 to Damascus had been hijacked. All passengers except the Jews and Israelis on board were released. Israel held its breath. Being a Jew and an Israeli, professor Samueloff was one of the hostages.

While working at the Bible shop and at home, I had fasted much for his release. Freed after ninety-nine days, he was asked what he did while held hostage. He told the press that while in prison (at that time in 1970), he had often sung Psalms and Händel's *Hallelujah Chorus*.

When we performed Händel's *Messiah* at Jerusalem's YMCA, I felt that having professor Samueloff tell his story there would bless all who knew of his capture and release. He and the choir leaders agreed, so he shared his experiences before our choir began its performance.

A short time later I visited the Samueloff family and saw how God continued to bless them. "You should write a book about your experiences, professor!" I encouraged him. Eventually, he did. The book is called *Ninety-nine Days in Damascus; The Story of Professor Shlomo Samueloff and the Hijack of TWA Flight 840 to Damascus*.

About forty years later, I sat in the balcony of Jerusalem's Clal building Pavilion auditorium, and listened to a choir from Norway singing Händel's *Messiah*. In my heart I heard the Hebrew translation of each English scripture that was sung. *This should be sung in Hebrew, and bless the Israelis!* I thought, and knew the time had come. I knew a musician who could do it - Arieh Bar David. I had hired him to teach music to my students at the Carmel School and he was now in the Philharmonic Orchestra. *Arieh will be the ideal conductor*, I thought. *I'll have to get a few like-minded people together to talk about this idea.*

Amikan Tavor was the one who had translated most of the *Messiah* text into a Hebrew version which sadly had never been returned after it was loaned out. Together with Efrat Gerlich who had the same vision, Amikam, Arieh and I met at Moshav Yad HaShmonah, near Jerusalem.

Amikan promised to work on the translation again, which was later perfected musically by Arieh. The next step was to recruit singers and musicians (especially those who knew Hebrew) and most importantly, finances to fund the project.

"I will participate generously!" Anita had assured us.

"We'd better hurry," Arieh joked, "Irene wants to hear the Hebrew version while she's still on earth to hear it. She'll be eighty-eight soon."

My heart's desire was fulfilled, even before my birthday. During Passover 2007, the first Hebrew performance of Händel's *Messiah - haMashiah* was performed in Jerusalem, at the Pavilion. I even had the privilege of singing alto in the choir. Because Arieh had other commitments, David Loden promised to continue the production.

Arieh Bar David (was Haimoff)
directing *Messiah*.

217

# 46

## Celebrate Life!

It was a joyous year in 2007, as Jerusalem celebrated her 40th anniversary as a unified city. There were dancing, singing and parades throughout the city. I celebrated my 88th birthday on August 25, 2008. The number 88 is associated with "resurrection". Taking stock of my life, I thanked the Lord for good health! Rarely did I have to pay a visit to a doctor or make use of my sick fund. Teaching still had my heart, and when people asked me about it, this continued to be my 'profession'. Even after having done this for so long, teaching Hebrew and sharing about the Heavenly roots from the Tenach continued to fill my heart with joy. Added to that was the privilege of sharing the beauty of Arabic words that were complimentary to the Hebrew language. More in the Word even than in the Land, I saw these Semitic roots of the sons of Shem as the true foundation for peace.

In the beginning of June 2009, during the same period as the Six Day War in 1967, I flew to California to see my sisters. After we've each led our interesting lives, with 'fruit' or results (physically or spiritually) God granted us to be together. Carol could only be there for a week, so I did likewise. Anita had invited me to join her on a longer trip, but financed this instead. All of us Poe girls were now in our 80's and 90's, near the 'sunset' time of our earthly lives, but each of us still in our right minds, and in fairly great health. A home town paper, the *Findlay Ohio* reported: "The five Poe sisters from way back in McComb, Ohio are all together!"

We enjoyed a special train ride, a gift from Aunt Naomi who couldn't participate in the reunion. How I thanked God for this time, and savored those six precious days. It had been like Israel's Six Day War – brief, but from God.

"*Kol yom veyom, bechol* **makome***, ken, hu yid'ag lekha!*" (God will take care of you in every **place!**), the Hebrew assembly in Jerusalem was singing before I

218

flew to the States. Upon my return to Israel, I was late for the meeting. When I entered the building, my mouth fell open when I heard the congregation sing, *"Kol yom veyom, bechol* **makome***, ken, hu yid'ag lekha!"* Again, God encouraged and reminded me that "Every day, in **every** place, God will take care of you!" He would continue to do so until I am with HIM – **THE** *Makome*!

Aunt Naomi treated my sisters and me to a Napa Valley Wine Train luncheon.

The felt olive tree I made for my mother's 80th birthday. From her, the 'good' Olive tree, came five branches.

# 47

## Glory and Honor to God – Forever!

"Now to the King eternal, immortal, invisible, the only wise God,
be honor and glory for ever and ever." 1 Timothy 1:17

In May of 2010, I saw my dream come to fruition once again when the Hebrew version of *Messiah - haMashiah*, was performed in three major cities in Israel. This time it was directed by David Loden.

"Are you interested in buying a ticket?" I asked everyone. "I've bought twenty, for then they only cost NIS 75 instead of NIS 90."

Most people couldn't let such a deal pass, so they bought my discount tickets. After these were sold, I immediately ordered another twenty tickets, believing I would sell those as well. After the third batch of twenty tickets, I was told to just write down the names of my contacts. "When they come to the performance," the organizers told me, "let them just say, 'I'm on Irene's list'. They'll pay less, even without that special ticket."

Finally, the day arrived for which I had waited with such longing and mounting excitement. Performances had already taken place in Kiryat Mozkin and at the Jaffa Music Center, but the highlight of the tour would be the three performances in Jerusalem on May 11, 12 and 13, 2010.

It was time for the performance to begin. The applause died down and the hall fell silent when Monica Meira Vasques picked up her conductor's baton. I closed my eyes when the Israel Chamber Orchestra began to play the overture and let the beautiful music, which I had heard so many times, caress my soul anew. What a wonderful moment when instead of "Comfort ye, Comfort ye My people", the tenor sang, *"Nachamu, nachamu Ami!"*

The powerful Hebrew Scriptures which several people and I had been working so hard to perfect, now filled the auditorium. The 'Liturgi-kal' Choir's jubilant voices filled the air with "The Glory of the Lord shall be revealed!" – Scripture most Jews know in Hebrew.

There were many Israelis in the auditorium, secular and religious, Jewish and Gentile believers. This time, nobody had to look up the meaning of the English words. In their own language they heard "With his stripes, we are healed". I could feel the evening going on forever. When the choir began to sing "Worthy is the Lamb that was slain", I had a glimpse of heaven. The performance ended with the glorious *Hallelujah Chorus*. "And He shall reign forever and ever!" - Händel's *haMashiah* had come to an end.

The public was ecstatic, and the conductor and soloists had to return three times to receive a standing ovation. At each performance, I was publicly honored by David Loden for my part in bringing this vision to fruition.

"Thank You Lord!" I raised my hand, to give glory to my Heavenly Father.

I am thrilled people now can order a DVD of this production!

# 48

## A Home in Jerusalem – My *Makome!*

The apartment on Narkis Street wasn't big, but for me it was perfect - centrally located and on the ground floor. Lou had found it, and it really had been a home to us. My heart sank when the owner's family informed me they wanted to sell it.

"You've rented faithfully all these years, so you'll have the first right of purchase," they said.

I never owned an apartment because both of my husbands felt that they were only pilgrims in this world. Neither did I have the money to buy it. The idea of having to move made me sad. *Perhaps somebody else will buy it for me and let me keep renting.* It was a hopeful thought. I shared my plight and the need of a miracle with my local assembly. "Please pray that the Lord will send a buyer for my apartment."

For most of my life, I had been on the move and often lived in very primitive circumstances. I was almost ninety years old, and preferred to stay in my small 'nest', surrounded by my books and belongings that held so many precious memories.

After the prayer meeting a Jewish believer, and very dear brother in the Lord said, "I'll buy the apartment for you." I could only praise God at the wonderful news, which was followed by another blessing. "You can live there for the same rent you're paying now, until the Lord calls you home."

"Thank You, Lord!" I clapped my hands. "And thank you!" I smiled at Shmuel Shmadja of Sar-El Tours. "And... there's no need to renovate the place. It would be hard to move all those books, papers and furniture around!" I added, relieved that he gave his assent.

Meeting with friends in the garden outside my apartment.

Blessed having a car, I always take people home after a service.
This car was provided by Anita. I'm sitting next to David Bogenreef, the beloved 'trumpeter'.

90th birthday blessings from the elders at the Messianic assembly, where I've been blessed many years. Also by their "Yanetz" Scriptural printing.

# 49

## Surrounded by a 'Cloud of Witnesses'

"Therefore, since we are surrounded by such a great cloud of witnesses, ... let us run with perseverance the race marked out for us." Hebrews 12:1 NIV

**The Berger brothers**
I met Reuven and Benjamin for the first time when they lived in Rosh Pina. I sometimes visit their meetings at Christ Church, Jerusalem.

**Rina Preiss**
Rina and I were like true sisters, and for years served together in homes, English meetings, Hebrew assemblies, and we distributed Scriptures together.

**Ruth Khoury**
Ruth is part of the Matar family who run a pharmacy inside Jaffa Gate. Stanley and I used to visit the Matar family in Nazareth. They were Arab believers who understood God's plan for Israel.

**Joseph Shulam**
Ada and I attended small group meetings at the home of Br. Shulam, who now has a meeting place close to where I live. I often visit the Netivya Hebrew fellowship and they have published stories about me in their magazine.

**Charles Kopp**
I first knew Charles from the Zion bookshop which was run by William Hull. Charles was also active in Arab outreach. Today, he is a well-known leader of the United Christian Council in Israel (U.C.C.I.) and pastor of Narkis Street Baptist Church.

## Hannah Hurnard
I met the famous author during united prayer meetings in Jerusalem and shared her books with many believers. I met with her again at her home in Poryah, near Tiberias.

## Ruth Dayan (wife of Moshe Dayan)
With Ruth I spoke about the work we did among Jewish and Arab schoolchildren, and the importance of youth coming together.

## Kaarlo Syvanto
I frequented the Syvantos' guesthouse in Tiberias and later the one they called The Hill. Kaarlo and I distributed Bibles in the north of Israel. I also worked with his sons Karlervo and Olavi.

## Dorothy Witner and Victoria Cheek
In the various places where Dorothy and Victoria lived, I often worked with them, assisting with women's and children's meetings.

## Lily Wreshner and Elsie Churcher
I knew them from Jerusalem and Haifa and stayed in their caravan overlooking Haifa Bay when they traveled abroad. I helped them with Bible distribution.

## Abu and his son Hanna
I knew 'Abu' and 'Im' for years before I understood that his name wasn't 'Abu Hanna', father of Hanna, but rather Wadia Saloom! Stanley spoke in many Arabic meetings in their Wadi Nisnas home in Haifa.

## Marcinkovskis
The couple were leaders of 'Bethesda' in Haifa. They served together with Dr.Pockroy and also Senya Rashelof of Nesher. We often held meetings in their home. Nellie and I held many children's meetings throughout the area.

## Mr. and Mrs. Moshe Ben Meir
In their home I attended my first Israeli Passover Seder. I had been in contact with them while still in the USA. I regularly visited them in their Haifa home, as he and the Birnbaums were connected to the Bible school in Haifa.

## Esther Dorflinger (now Korson)
I often had fellowship in Esther's tea rooms. On my 80th birthday, she hosted a real 'splash'!

### Vera Swartztrauber
Vera had worked in Es-Salt, Jordan, and later came to Israel. She and I often went to a Christian school in Ramallah where we spoke about the importance of the Jewish-Arab connection through the Scriptures.

### Heinz and Gavriella Pollack
Gavriella and I rented a room in Motza, and later I visited them in Talpiot, until they moved to the Eben Haezer Home in Haifa. I taught their son's family Hebrew.

### Moshe Ben Shmuel
Moshe had escaped the Holocaust. Together with Orville Wallace he hosted Shabbat evening meetings. Moshe became famous for playing the accordion and I often took people to their gatherings.

### Chris and Elmer Josephson
Chris and Elmer's love for Israel and the Bible bound us together. I helped them find apartments in Ramallah and Jerusalem. Together we distributed *Bible Light* and Scripture booklets.

### Jacob Gartenhaus
I often drove the Gartenhaus family around while they were in Israel.

### 'Scoop' Wilson
'Scoop' and Dorothy were friends from the US. I often joined them when they assisted the staff of Ulpan Akiva in Netanya, where Shulamit Katznelson was in charge.

### Derek Prince and Lance Lambert
I often took others to the meetings of these special speakers, and translated when needed. Derek Prince went home to be with the Lord; Lance Lambert is still a popular speaker in Israel today.

### Saleem Hilwe
Saleem came from Kfar Yassif, near Acre, and was Stanley's 'spiritual son'.

# 50

## Watching God Lead - To Jerusalem in the Middle East

"As for me being on the way, the Lord led..." Genesis 24:27

The above verse is one of my favorite Scriptures. When we start out, we never know where the Lord is going to lead. But as we go along, He drops things in our laps and leads us. We need to trust not man, but God.

A lot of things I never planned, but they simply came my way by our faithful abiding Holy Spirit. I went to Bible school feeling I had a burden for India. However, the love and burden for Israel that came to me was, and remains, unshakable. There were, however, touches of India and other lands interspersed.

The Lord has supplied all my needs. "Seek ye first the Kingdom of God", and don't worry about organizations! It seems that God's one Scriptural organization is the local church to which any believer can belong. I believe that the true body of Messiah should show a oneness. First of all, I'm a fervent believer in the importance of fellowshipping with believers in one's neighborhood. Like a week-long "kibbutz", we Bible believers should help and care for each other, especially in times of war, persecution, or when there is a shortage of gas and cars.

Reconciliation is something I strongly believe in. We should be doing all we can to bless the Jewish people and then we shall be blessed in return, but not only the Jewish people! By visiting the local Arabic and Messianic congregations, we form relationships and begin to see our common roots. When we focus on our love for the Messiah and what we have in common, rather than what separates us, we can begin to build bridges of understanding, rather than walls of separation.

Every week, I study the Scriptures in my congregation and take part in regular prayer meetings. God has given me the blessing of being with and helping many special people, a number of whom stayed in one of my guest apartments, or came to visit our home.

I continue to distribute monthly prayer letters for *Voice of the Martyrs* which was begun by the Wurmbrands, who are now with the Lord. The VOM now publishes a colorful magazine. For years now, I have promoted this important work of bringing to the church's attention the needs of world-wide believers who are persecuted.

Teaching Hebrew in the lounge of the Baptist Church across the street from where I live continues to be one of my favorite activities. I use my famous cloth on which I printed Scriptures and my grammar charts, as well as poems, songs, the weekly Parasha and an easy Hebrew newspaper to open the world of Hebrew to my students, some of whom are transient. Some of them come even if they are in an Ulpan! Because the lessons are free, many are interested to give it a try. And wherever I go, there is always someone who cries out, "Oh, I was in your Hebrew class at such and such a time…!"

I guess being related to Edgar Allan Poe genetically predisposed me to writing poems and songs. Mine, however, are always on spiritual subjects. Writing has become part of my God-given ministry. These include regular, circular letters abroad, articles, poems and Biblical teachings, called *midrasheem*.

When I was born, my mother blessed me by giving me a name with a beautiful spiritual meaning. Her name was Olive, and for her 80th birthday I made a felt tree with five branches, symbolizing her five daughters. Not only was I physically "planted into that good olive tree", but spiritually as well. According to Romans 11, I have been grafted into the Good Olive Tree and the Messiah (Christ), given through the Jews.

At my father's funeral, the mourners sang "God will take care of you!" My heavenly Father has fulfilled that promise - not only in McComb, Ohio, where we then lived, but also in Jerusalem and everywhere in between. God has never let me down. I have stumbled many times, but He sustained me. I know that He will continue to take care of me until He calls me, Irene (Peace) to the heavenly Place. Then I will see Him, Who is called *Ha Makome* – **THE** Place!

# EPILOGUE

## From the Author

It was Wende Carr who had begun to collect the material needed to write Irene's story. Unable to tackle the project herself, she felt God prompting her to approach me. It was in the last days of December 2009, that Wende, Irene and I met to discuss the project. This is what Irene said,

"Friends have been urging me for some time to write a book about my life, but I didn't like the idea." She shook her head. "My ego will get in the way and bookshops are already filled with rows and rows of books. Anyway, nowadays TV and the computer take precedence over reading books. Also, I don't have the funds to pay for the printing cost." She laughed. "Who is going to promote my book? Am I supposed to do that myself? No, I still don't think people will be interested in reading about my life. What is so special about it after all? True, I serve the God of Israel, but aren't all believers supposed to be servants and witness to His greatness and goodness?"

The 'book idea' was placed on the backburner, but behind the scenes, God put His plan in motion. Still a novice writer, I proudly held my diploma from a course called 'Shape, Write and Sell your Novel'. It was dated August 25, 2008, the exact date of Irene's 88th birthday! Two years later, I was asked to use my honed skills to write the story of Irene's life.

"Who am I, but one who has seen His unchangeable love?" Irene said when we talked about how to write her life-story. It was a rather overwhelming project to her.

For me, the challenge began to write a book about this remarkable, unique, ninety-one-year old woman of God. I'd only occasionally seen Irene in passing, so I didn't know what I had gotten myself into.

Writing her story became an exciting journey and what struck me was that, despite Irene's degrees and endless list of achievements, she has always stayed real. Everything she did for others, she did as unto the Lord. Christ was first in her life, and therefore everything else fell into proper focus. Even today, Irene's life is an adventure of faith and joy. To her, JOY is – Jesus first, Others next, Yourself last.

I thank God for the privilege of getting to know Irene in this unique way, and for the honor of writing about her amazing life. Touched by the Savior's resurrection power, this ordinary girl acquired extraordinary potential.

The reason Irene agreed to have this book written is to give glory to God. Our prayer is that people will be touched by the story of one woman who gave her life over to God – because He could do more with it than she, who feels herself so unworthy.

Irene will stay in her armor to the last, of that I'm certain. And when the Lord calls her home, she will be welcomed with the words:

**"Well done, good and faithful servant of God.**
**Enter into your eternal rest."**

During a 2011 Valentine's lunch with Hela and Petra, the writer.

# APPENDIX

# *The Holy City* - A Hymn

Lyrics: Frederick Weatherly, 1892
Music: Michael Maybrick

Last night I lay a-sleeping
There came a dream so fair,
I stood in old Jerusalem
Beside the temple there.
I heard the children singing,
And ever as they sang,
Me thought the voice of angels
From heaven in answer rang.

**Jerusalem! Jerusalem!**
**Lift up your gates and sing,**
**Hosanna in the highest!**
**Hosanna to your King!**

And then me thought my dream
was changed,
The streets no longer rang,
Hushed were the glad
Hosannas
The little children sang.
The sun grew dark with
mystery,
The morn was cold and chill,
As the shadow of a cross arose
Upon a lonely hill.

**Jerusalem! Jerusalem!**
**Hark! How the angels sing,**
**Hosanna in the highest!**
**Hosanna to your King!**

And once again the scene was
changed;
New earth there seemed to be;
I saw the Holy City
Beside the tide-less sea;
The light of God was on its
streets,
The gates were open wide,
And all who would might enter,
And no one was denied.
No need of moon or stars by
night,
Or sun to shine by day;
It was the new Jerusalem
That would not pass away.

**Jerusalem! Jerusalem!**
**Sing for the night is o'er!**
**Hosanna in the highest!**
**Hosanna for evermore!**

During my forty-day fast in Beersheva I translated this hymn into
Hebrew, adding one verse concerning the Jerusalem Millennium.
Amikan perfected my Hebrew.

# Hanukah and Christmas
by Irene Levi

"A great miracle was here"
At Hanukah, we say each year.
What miracle Messiah's birth
Who, by a virgin, came to earth. (Isaiah 7:14)

Feast of lights: eight lights relate
How oil for one night burned for eight.
The Light to Gentiles, twith Israel,
Shines forth - His Name, "Emmanuel". (Isaiah 42:6)

Enemies ruled in the land
Until arose that mighty band.
"The Mighty God", a Son, was given
To save from Satan unto Heaven. (Isaiah 9:6)

In the temple, at this feast,
Jesus walked where Maccabee
Dedicated the house of stone.
He's the Temple built by God alone. (John 10:22)

Hasmoneans the altar cleansed
To worship God the way He'd planned.
Jesus cleansed the altar twice,
Became our Altar-Sacrifice. (Isaiah 53)

I'm now His miracle, temple, light,
A pure and living sacrifice.
With those of old, we'll conquerors be,
With God, against one enemy.

# Bird's Eye View of Israel's History

With the fall of Jerusalem in 70 AD, most of the Jews were dispersed through-out the world. In the centuries that followed Roman rule, Palestine, so named by the Romans, passed from one conqueror to another – Byzantines, Crusad-ers, and Muslims. For 400 long years, the land of Israel was a tiny province of the mighty Ottoman (Turkish) rulers. Wherever the Jews found a new place to live, the longing to return to their homeland was always kept alive. The Dias-pora Jews kept believing that one day, their God-given Land would be re-deemed.

While working as a journalist in Paris since 1891, Theodor Herzl, a Hungarian-born Jew, witnessed the anti-Semitism at the time of the Dreyfus case. He espoused the idea of a Jewish nation, and saw the need for the return of the Jews to Palestine on a massive scale – from all the countries of the Dias-pora. In 1897, Herzl opened the First Zionist Congress in Basle, Switzerland. In his diary, he wrote: "At Basle I founded the Jewish State.... Perhaps in five, and certainly in fifty, everyone will know it."

Zionism, born in the 19th century, was a political movement that be-lieved in the return of the Jewish people to Zion – meaning Jerusalem and the Land of Israel. The 1882 pogroms, anti-semitism and economic hardship brought on wave after wave of *Aliyah* (literally "going up). What awaited the immigrants wasn't exactly a "land of milk and honey". For centuries, the land had been neglected and was under populated. "... A desolated country whose soil is rich enough, but is given over wholly to weeds – a silent mournful ex-panse...," Mark Twain wrote in 1869.

Plots of often swampy land were bought by the Jewish National Fund and by zealous motivation, hard work and enormous sacrifice, turned into pro-ductive farmland. Not only Jews immigrated to the land of Israel. From the surrounding countries, Arabs too began to arrive and settle down, mostly for economic reasons.

After the defeat of the Turks, Palestine came under British Mandate in 1917. At first, they brought stability, and with the Balfour Declaration, the new rulers seemed sympathetic to Zionist aims. When the Nazis came to power in 1933, many European Jews fled to Palestine. Towns flourished and 'tower and stockade' settlements sprang up all over the country. "Disturbances", the Brit-ish called the increasing murderous Arab riots. After almost thirty years of rul-ing Mandatory Palestine, the British were fed up. They didn't want to deal with the Arab-Jewish strife any longer. The 'problem' of Palestine was put before the UN.

After the UN vote in November of 1947, which approved the formation of a Jewish homeland on the land of Israel, spasmodic fighting had become a full-fledged war. Arab military units from Syria, Iraq and Egypt were determined to drive the Jews from their promised State. Jerusalem was besieged, and during the six weeks before the British were scheduled to leave, the Arabs fought hard to gain as much territory as possible.

Biblical prophecies were fulfilled when on May 15, 1948, the State of Israel was declared.

Map of Israel in the 1950's

# My Deep Burden for His Church

A practical pattern for moving toward that unity for which many pray, especially for Jerusalem. He enables!

**PRAY** for the **PEACE** of Jerusalem, especially in the Prince of Peace.

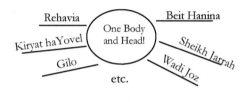

Manifested first where we live, caring for needs, assembling as 'kibbutz'. Jerusalem divided by areas, place (as Haifa and Jerusalem, Ephesus and Smyrna.) "On earth as in Heaven". On the North are three gates, on the South three, etc. An angel at each gate of the Church of Sheikh Jarrah, of Rehaviah, etc. Each gate a pearl. As the USA ~ separated states in each place. As Israel ~ localizing of Jews scattered in nations, so believers from denominations in every place, ready for going to one Place. One Temple of living stones where we **are**. His *Mishkan* (Tabernacle), the *Shekinah* (Presence) in each *Shekhuna* (community). "One in Spirit," but the Body perfected too. Learn in healthy Body cells (lest in prison cells). Not our 'choosing' (cliques) but we all His Chosen, as twelve disciples, as a family-made of all kinds under 'one roof'. The strong help the weak. Membership in the same Book of Life, but we 'belong' where we live. May what is GOOD be in every part, not special groups doing special things. Local church His one N.T. 'organization', name of **place** – only designations. Keep Jerusalem ONE, help our area – true autonomy! Save GAS in energy crisis – even walk ( as on Yom Kippur). Meet in homes (in turn?) not religious buildings, as families, in simplicity. Share facilities and in cars to city wide meetings, shopping, etc. One rule for marriage: both believers learn to adjust. God is called "The PLACE". May He rule in each location, not in 'two states' (in Israel.)

**OH, JERUSALEM**, put on your beautiful garments… out of ashes (past).

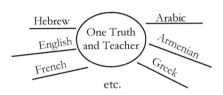

His Word the same for all, but expressed in different languages with culture which clothes it (original songs, holidays, symbols, nuances hard to translate). Language 'problem' of Jerusalem, its blessing: a better way of 'division' into city-wide meetings (staggered times, all ours). Go to where hear best in uninterrupted flow in teaching, prayer (where one can understand, say Amen), testimony, as one choir (sing same words.) In Israel, HEBREW renewed (Scriptures source) its greatest blessing. ARABIC, Semitic, is nearest and can be blessed by this fact; in 'Jerusalem United', in freedom of assembly. Visit each other's meetings, learn language, culture. Thus locally led, autonomous (through help from abroad.) In Jerusalem, already 'International', also our English, French, German, Armenian, Greek, Russian 'nests' for ones coming up to worship, share, send out streams of blessing to the world. As radio news: different languages at different times, all 'belong to all'. Bigger buildings used, forgetting past 'tags'. Elders, apostles… in leadership times according to language, for prayer and planning for general meetings. Babel turned to blessing in Truth expressed in every tongue. Not divide on certain truths known, best to share and help **all** to grow. No foreign heads, but the Holy Spirit and His whole Word guide, to His Truth, for us, here. Communication, better division than age, race, level of spiritual maturity. Make **every** week a holy week by **our** united language meetings at different, best suited times.

All, His ambassadors, 'embassy'. This even while denominational and organizational division still going on, unless…

**OH, JERUSALEM** how often I would have gathered you together…

One GOD to PRAISE

'Euro-vision', a pattern for 'Yeru-shalayim', Uru-shaleem, Jerusalem vision'. Great that Israel won on "Hallelu-ya". Let's go on singing in different languages, not for contests but for praise of the great King, Lord God of Israel, at time best suited. (Sunday p.m?) Each could take prepared song sheets in his language and follow meanings on weekly contributions from our language gatherings or from aboard. E.g. Hebrew chorus, Arab solo, French duet, Armenian choir, Finnish with costumes, German with instruments, even dance, all to glorify Him and bless ones attending. At this time all could sing together or in turn their translation of famous songs, Lord's Prayer. No speakers (needing translation). Comments of blessing or criticism could be made on song sheet, to return to singers for blessing or improving. What joy, ones from the nations coming to Jerusalem to bless and be blessed in every tongue and song-fest in all the languages, esp. Hebrew and Arabic, in united Jerusalem. 'U.N.' at its best! Taste of the millennium! Specials coming to Jerusalem for **their** program could best fit into such regular frameworks, **led by Jerusalem elders** ('in one accord in one place') and contributing to rent of the best suited buildings. Like-wise for other cities. Not just at 'feast'. May JERUSALEM be an example for other cities in (1) community **caring**, (2) language gatherings in the **Word,** (3) songs **together.**

---

*God's "Shecina"*
on every *shecuna* (area)
to bless our *shecaneem*
(neighbors)
God's real *Mishkan*
(Tabernacle) is seen
One temple here
God's Presence very near
Thou Prince of Peace
appear In Israel.
The Word became flesh
and *shacan* among us.

I took Solomon Ostrovsky, who by then was about 99 years old, on a tour of Jerusalem. He couldn't believe his eyes, how it had grown.

Sharon Sanders, me and Hela Crown Tamir, during my 91st birthday party at Beit Ticho, in August 2010.